LOVE IS
ALL AROUND
IN DISGUISE

LOVE IS
ALL AROUND
IN DISGUISE
MEDITATIONS FOR
SPIRITUAL SEEKERS

IRENE DUGAN, R.C., AND AVIS CLENDENEN

CHIRON PUBLICATIONS · NEW YORK

Chiron Publications, New York, N.Y.
Copyright © 2004 by Chiron Publications
All rights reserved. Published 2004
Printed in the United States of America

ISBN 1-888602-29-5

In memory of Tommy Dugan

The quality of a life means more than its duration. Like his grandaunt Sister Irene, our Tommy enjoyed life to its fullest and in turn shared his vitality with all who knew him.

Tom and Mary Dugan

To the bereft of the world who have not known love or kindness. May they find their way into the heart of God.

-Irene Dugan, r.c.

pro omnibus sororibus misericordiae

Contents

Foreword

I DID NOT HAVE THE OPPORTUNITY TO WORK WITH SISTER IRENE DUGAN, r.c., but all of us now have the privilege of coming to know her and work with her through the legacy of this book of hers, *Love Is All Around in Disguise: Meditations for Spiritual Seekers*, lovingly edited by Avis Clendenen.

One event recalled by Terence Mickey sums up for me an essential quality of Irene Dugan's life. Mickey speaks of "Aunt Judy" (as he knew his great-aunt) with a group of children around her as she held a plush bunny rabbit with long ears. She bent one of the long ears down over the chest of the bunny and asked, "Do you know why the bunny has such long ears?" She answered her own question. "So that he can listen to his heart." Irene Dugan was a woman who listened to her heart. Through her heart she entered into the Spiritual Exercises of St. Ignatius Loyola and into Dr. Ira Progoff's *At a Journal Workshop: Writing to Access the Power of the Unconscious and Evoke Creative Ability*. As a result, the manuscript Dugan entrusted to Avis Clendenen provides us with ways of listening to our hearts. For in this book she has written exercises for the heart.

Dr. Ira Progoff paid Irene Dugan the ultimate compliment when he told her that she was "a very wise old woman and a very wise old man." Although she was about seventy at the time, the emphasis was not on age, but on the wisdom of human integration. Because she was a seeker, she found her quest for greater authenticity, spiritual depth, and self-realization in an especially rich way in the prayer exercises of Ignatius Loyola integrated with the holistic depth psychology of Ira Progoff. In her own life of ministry, she showed how others might enter into the way that Ignatius Loyola and Ira Progoff had mentored for her.

The book of Spiritual Exercises was the result of "notes" that Ignatius Loyola had made about his reading and about his experiences, reflecting on and "noting" his interior movements. I think that Irene Dugan follows in the footsteps of Ignatius in her own note-taking, which eventually resulted in this book. Drawing particularly upon the kind of reflections called for in Progoff's work, Dugan puts together a carefully interwoven whole from the contributions of this sixteenth-century saint and this twentieth-century psychologist. Her book, then, becomes the foundation for our own "noting" what is the "thread of continuity" that ties together the whole of our life.

Ignatius Loyola deliberately wrote an exercise book, an educational tool that necessarily involves its reader. Ira Progoff, in his workshops and conferences and in his various books, always entered his listeners and readers into the activity of their own journaling. True to those who were her mentors, Irene Dugan has written a book that stimulates and guides our own activity as we seek and find our way "into the heart of God." This book cannot be read; it demands our exercising.

I will be forever grateful that Dugan found in my translation and "reading" of the Spiritual Exercises a stimulus for writing these meditations for spiritual seekers. Besides interweaving the Ignatian material with written exercises inspired by select insights from Ira Progoff, Dugan had added her own "Fifth Week" to the traditional four weeks of the Spiritual Exercises in a chapter she titled "The Woman." Her own originality and genius shine out as she sums up the wholeness of the human being, imaginatively reflected in Mary of Nazareth in her relationship with God.

Let me also express my gratitude to Avis Clendenen, who invited me to write this foreword. Because of her own labor of love in producing this book, I found it a joy and an honor to play my little part, to be among "the seekers, flounderers, stargazers, and lovers" identified with Irene Dugan, r.c.

David L. Fleming, SJ

In Remembrance

by Terence Mickey

SISTER IRENE DUGAN, R.C., WAS MY GREAT-AUNT, BUT I KNEW HER ALWAYS
as Aunt Judy. Martin Buber, a Jewish theologian who influenced my
great-aunt, taught that all of life is rooted in relationships. He
believed that sometimes we understand something just by meeting
someone, that there are some people in whose presence we find ourselves incapable of any kind of falsehood, and my Aunt Judy was one
of these rare people. Despite the cottony white hair, the soft voice,
and the baby powder scent when she hugged you, you weren't in
Judy's presence long before you felt and understood an undeniable
force to be reckoned with. I only shared her company a handful of
times, but the occasions were all memorable.

When asked to write an introduction to Judy's book, I first ques-
tioned my credentials. There are other family members who knew
her better, who spent more time in her company, who may have
openly received her encouragement, or begrudgingly accepted her
setting them straight, more often than I had the opportunity to –
her eight sisters and brothers, for instance, or any of the thirty-two
nieces and nephews she kept in touch with over the telephone and
in letters. I was sure anyone would do a better job. Then I thought
of Aunt Judy, what advice she would offer me. "Why not you," I
imagined her saying, prodding me with her bristly encouragement.
"You're a writer. So write. What you don't know, you'll find out.
Pick up the pen already. Come on. Get going. Write!" It is with her
constant support and loving push that I write this introduction.

My great-aunt Kathleen had two wedding cakes: one cake baked
for the day of her wedding on September 11, 1948, and one for the

night before. She and her fiancé, Bud, drove into Manhattan to celebrate with her sister, Judy, semicloistered at the time and living at the Cenacle on Riverside Drive. The image of a newlywed couple, decked out in a regal gown and black tuxedo, with a three-tier cake, and a room packed with giddy nuns – every one of them wielding a silver fork – was unforgettable for Kathleen, as were most visits the family took to see Judy. Judy's mother and father and her four brothers and four sisters would all cram into the Packard and head out to the Cenacle in Lake Ronkonkoma for the day. Kathleen remembers the nuns feeding the kids ice cream and cookies, and how she and her siblings would try for a glimpse of the clothesline, to solve, once and for all, the mystery of what the Sisters wore underneath their habits. The demands of the semi-cloistered life – solitude and separation – made each visit to see Judy an adventure, something rare to be thankful for and cherished, but the commitment she made to God and the Sisters of the Cenacle was at times difficult for her family, especially in the beginning.

When Aunt Judy entered the Cenacle in 1930, she was twenty-one years old. Her mother had the hardest time with Judy's decision. Judy was the oldest of nine and often helped with the cooking and tutored her younger brothers and sisters in their school subjects. She was an asset during hard times, and her mother didn't want to lose her. Her father had said he knew once Judy left, she'd never come back.

Perhaps what her mother feared and respected most in her daughter was the conviction she had inherited. The women were more outspoken than the men in the Dugan family, and Judy, like her mother, was not afraid to say what she thought. Judy always enjoyed the story of how her mother chewed out a police officer for complaining about the family dog. "Don't you have any criminals to chase?" her mother said to the young man. "Don't you have something better to do besides worrying about a harmless dog?" Then she shut the front door in the officer's stunned face. Judy was determined and she knew, without anyone's counsel, what she wanted. She had intended to enter the Sisters of Charity, but shortly before she was to do so the nuns sent Judy to a retreat at the

Cenacle. It was on this retreat that she decided the Cenacle suited her better than the Sisters of Charity; Judy was a Sister of the Cenacle for sixty-seven years.

If not for my Aunt Judy I wouldn't have known the overwhelming size and presence of my extended family. Judy organized two family reunions – for her fiftieth jubilee as a Sister of the Cenacle and for her eightieth birthday. On both occasions the Dugans overcrowded the Cenacle. Aunt Judy was the anchor for three generations of the Dugan family. My mother remembers the only occasion she saw all of her cousins was when Aunt Judy invited the family to the Cenacle for a special event. She also remembers Aunt Judy present at every significant celebration in her life – her graduation, her wedding, and especially when she needed counsel. I remember Aunt Judy as a constant reminder of our roots, our history, of one another, a touchstone for what was possible and within our grasp if we were willing to work hard enough and reach.

The last time I saw Aunt Judy she was sitting in the basement of the Fullerton Cenacle, telling stories. She was a wise and careful storyteller. She had excellent vision, a talent for picking out and describing the most telling detail; with this detail and the conviction in her voice, she always commanded your full attention. In the basement of the Cenacle, she was telling the story of her sister Ida May's death at age six months of influenza. Judy rode with her father in a horse-drawn carriage to deliver the coffin to the burial. She remembered when they hit a pothole in the road and the small coffin jumped and the baby's body made a quick knocking sound. Her father turned to her and said, "Don't tell your mother what you just heard." The room let out a gasp as Judy continued, already into another story. She had an unflinching eye, and she wanted to experience life as it was, which carried over into her stories.

At the end of her storytelling in the Cenacle basement, she picked up a stuffed bunny rabbit sitting at her feet. She pulled the long ear of the rabbit down over his chest and said, "This rabbit has long ears. Does anyone know why?" The room shook their heads, eagerly awaiting the answer, and Judy said, "This rabbit has long ears so he can listen to his heart."

I hadn't known my grandmother and Aunt Judy even had a sister named Ida May, which revealed to me how much of a historian Aunt Judy was for the Dugan family. When my Aunt Mary was in nursing school, she had to do a presentation on a family theorist, using the study of her own family as a model. She called Aunt Judy first. Aunt Judy mailed her a recording of what she knew and began the tape by saying, "If you had been paying attention at the last family reunion, you would know that . . . ."

A few days before her death, I mailed my aunt a thank-you letter. She had sent me a copy of *Letters to a Young Poet* by Rilke and a short note, which read: "No writer should be without Rilke's letters." I was in graduate school at the time, and I didn't get around to thanking her until July, when I'd finished everything for school, moved into a new apartment, and settled into post-graduate life. She never did receive my letter. My grandmother, Judy's youngest sister, brought the letter back with her from Chicago, still sealed in the envelope, the red postmark stamped proof of delivery. She handed me the thank you I'd written two weeks earlier, along with Judy's letter opener. A gift for me, she said, something she knew Judy would want me to have. "So you remember her," my grandmother said to me. "Yes, there is so much to remember," I thought to myself.

How rarely we meet someone who has watched the world as closely as she, who has ruminated on love and faith with as much focus and insight as her, who was willing to share her wisdom with anyone who would listen. What makes Rilke's letters exceptional is the abundance of insight in Rilke's looking back on his own life in order to help a young poet start his. Judy possessed the same intro- and retrospection. Her advice never simply considered the now, but possessed an intelligence of the past and future as well.

One year after her death, I met a priest in Vermont, Father James Nielson, who by coincidence had been to the Fullerton Cenacle for a retreat. He had been preparing for the priesthood when he met Judy, and he said to me, "If your aunt hadn't joined the Cenacle, Terence, she would have raised serious hell in the corporate world." *They were the same to all people* is a phrase often used by my family, and many would agree that it is custom-made for Aunt Judy. She never compromised herself or acted in any way she didn't mean to act. But her hardnosed observations and attitude served a much loftier and nobler purpose than what is found in the corporate world. *Love Is All Around in Disguise*, my great-aunt's legacy realized in print, generously reveals her purpose: to enter, without fear, "the process of striving toward wholeness and holiness," a lifelong journey for my Aunt Judy.

There is only one single way. Go into yourself. Investigate the reason that bids you write . . . . And if out of this turning inward, out of this sinking into your own world verses come, then it will not occur to you to ask any one whether they are good verses. Nor will you try to interest magazines in your poems: for you will see in them your fond natural possession, a fragment and a voice of your life. A work of art is good if it has sprung from necessity. In this nature of its origin lies its judgment; there is no other.

    —Rainer Maria Rilke

       (from *Letters to a Young Poet*, pp. 16–18)

Preface

We've been reading the Book of Sirach, which is one of the Wisdom books of the Bible. There's one phrase that stuck with me. (You could stay for months on one phrase.) And the one phrase that stuck with me is "cling to God" (Sir. 2:3 NRSV). So what does it mean to cling to God? It means to be always present and aware God is present in every moment of every day surrounding us, in us . . . .

Greatness is for each of us – the potential for fulfilling ourselves. The real greats have faced the risk and gone with it. And the halfway greats didn't make the right turn in the road. Sometimes we miss the boat – and it's very sad to miss the boat. I hope I haven't – but I'm still paddling away . . . .

—interview with Irene Dugan, r.c., May 1997

IRENE DUGAN WAS BORN IN 1909 IN NEW YORK CITY. IN 1930 SHE entered the international Roman Catholic community of women known as the Religious of the Cenacle. The Cenacle sisters dedicate themselves to the ministries of spiritual care and companioning, teaching the art forms of prayer and interior growth, and guiding souls through days of reflection and retreat experiences. Their name is biblically based in the post-resurrection and ascension narratives in which the followers of Jesus struggled to discern the meaning of all the things that had gone on (Luke 24:13–35). The inspiration for the Sisters of the Cenacle's life of prayer, community, and service to the spiritual ministries springs from the first cenacle where the apostles and some women, including Mary, prayed in the *coenaculum* (cenacle) for the outpouring of the spirit promised by Jesus. The Acts of the Apostles (1:12–14) record their gathering in the cenacle, or upper room, so that "with one accord they devoted themselves to prayer."

Irene Dugan professed her perpetual vows with the Religious of the Cenacle in 1938 when she was twenty-nine years old, and she lived her life intensely present, clinging to God until her death at age eighty-seven in July of 1997. She was a teacher, director of retreats, spiritual guide, and pioneer in depth spirituality – the blending of the traditions of Christian spirituality with modern holistic depth psychology and the arts. The innovative spiritual growth groups for laywomen she began in 1946 continued as women's spirituality groups until the time of her death.

In the early 1970s her interest in psychospiritual integration led her to invite Dr. Ira Progoff, the originator of the *Intensive Journal*® method, to give *Intensive Journal*® workshops at the Cenacle Retreat House on Chicago's south side, his first introduction in the Midwest. Sister Dugan became a Progoff *Intensive Journal*® consultant, conducting innovative workshops throughout the United States and in England, Ireland, Scotland, and France.

Irene Dugan and Ira Progoff shared a warm and abiding friendship for more than a quarter of a century. Irene told me that Ira once said of her that "she was a very wise woman and a very wise man." Irene shared this memory with me not long before her death, saying, "this is what we are all supposed to become if we have truly lived." The recollection brought her joy. Irene Dugan placed her spiritual gifts at the disposal of those she guided and, when necessary, chided them on their journey into the realms of the inner world and its workings.

Irene dedicated many years to exploring the integration of the Spiritual Exercises of St. Ignatius, the sixteenth-century founder and spiritual animator of the Society of Jesus, with holistic depth psychology. She employed these insights in her ministry of spiritual mentoring because she believed Ignatius and Progoff provided contemporary spiritual seekers with methods for growth in self-knowledge central to becoming whole human beings *and* experiencing friendship with God.

The vision of a more holistic approach to spiritual growth and human development led her and Rev. Paul Robb, SJ, to cofound the Institute for Spiritual Leadership (ISL) in Chicago in the early 1970s as a training program for men and women seeking knowledge and skill in the art forms of holistic spiritual direction. With over seven hundred alums from more than forty countries, the ISL continues to thrive today, still holding to the conviction that only as spiritual leaders come to know themselves and their own journeys intimately can they claim to be able to companion others on the sacred and scary journey of spiritual life and growth.

In 1983, Sister Dugan became a scholar-in-residence at the Institute of Pastoral Studies of Loyola University in Chicago. She taught graduate-level courses in spirituality and provided spiritual direction for graduate students, while continuing her women's spiritual growth groups, providing spiritual direction for private clients, and giving retreats. Loyola University recognized Sister Dugan with an honorary doctorate in 1987.

My own history with Sister Irene Dugan began in 1971 when I was twenty-one years old and in search of a spiritual mentor. She served as my spiritual guide for twenty-six years. My last conversation with Irene took place in June 1997, a few weeks before her death. She directed me to pick up a box she left for me at the Fullerton Cenacle, but made no mention of its contents. The box contained two copies of her unfinished manuscript, an audio recording of her introduction to the book, and assorted notes and papers. Thus I became a trustee of *Love Is All Around in Disguise*, the title Irene had given to her book.

I wish to honor Irene's chosen title by briefly exploring my sense of her original intent. The notions of love surrounding us in disguise and of life as an adventure of endless discovery are threads in Irene's unique philosophy of taking the risk to live life to the fullest, of not missing the boat. Her choice of title led me to re-read an article written by one of St. Ignatius's sons, Jesuit theologian Karl Rahner, SJ. In "The Hiddenness of Being" (1969a, chapter 6), Rahner posits that our individual openness to God is a question of our own self-determination. Each human being stands in free love before the God of a possible revelation. It is God's deepest desire to disclose God's Self as a gift of love to God's creatures, made in the Creator's own image and likeness. This gift is available to us to the extent that we open ourselves to receive it. Rahner says that we can hear God's message when we do not, on account of wrongly directed love, narrow the horizon of our own spiritual possibilities, that is, when we do not make it impossible for the word of God to be heard in us, to "tell us under what *guise* God wishes to encounter us" (McCool 1975, p. 45; italics mine). The First Epistle of John (4:16) records that God is love. This God who is love desires to find a home – to abide – in us. Such love is all around in disguise awaiting our discovery.

Those who experienced working with Irene in her most treasured course, "The Inner World and Its Workings," will find their memories stirred by the material in this book. In putting together this book, it has been my challenge and graced opportunity to respect her voice and unique expressions in bringing to fruition this singular aspect of her spiritual legacy, *Love Is All Around in Disguise: Meditations for Spiritual Seekers*. This book joins *Spirituality in Depth: Essays in Honor of Sister Irene Dugan, r.c.* (Clendenen 2002) as a companion piece for those seeking a fuller share in the greatness – the potential for fulfilling ourselves – that Irene believed is our destiny.

Avis Clendenen

Acknowledgments

. . . from the water . . .

. . . the heavens were opened . . .

. . . the Spirit of God descending . . .

. . . a voice . . .

THESE ARE PHRASES FROM THE GOSPEL OF MATTHEW DESCRIBING THE scene of the baptism of Jesus in the Jordan. This ancient myth contains the powerful vision linking earthly elements to divine manifestation. The Spirit of God descends like a dove, alights on Jesus as he wades in the waters of the Jordan, and "a voice from heaven speaks." Jesus "inhears" the voice saying, "This is . . . my beloved with whom I am well pleased" (Mt. 3:16–17 NRSV).

The term used in the text for such a voice is what the rabbis called a *batqôl,* literally meaning "the daughter of a voice," that is, a little voice or whisper. The ancients understood such a voice to be an agent of revelation. I came to understand this passage in a new way as I experienced Irene Dugan's *batqôl* rising up from the text and wafting about my life as I worked with her to bring this book to print.

We have so many to thank for their patient, careful, and continuous contributions to the realization of *Love Is All Around in Disguise: Meditations for Spiritual Seekers.*

The seemingly endless largesse of Irene's dear friend Barbara Howard and the Howard Family Foundation is the bedrock of the Sister Irene Dugan, r.c., Legacy Project. Our gratitude is immeasurable.

From the beginning, Chiron Publications owner and publisher Murray Stein believed Irene's transformational presence would linger on this side to ripen our souls. This book is another dancing butterfly gently matured through his trust and attention.

In his remembrance, Terence spoke eloquently for all of the very large Dugan clan. And with her religious family, the Sisters of the Cenacle of the North American Province, you all provided emotional, spiritual, financial and intellectual support over the course of these past seven years. Your genuine interest in seeing this work come to fruition was fuel on a sometimes-arduous journey.

Special note must be made of the Sisters of the Cenacle at the Fullerton and Warrenville Cenacles in Illinois, especially Sisters Marguerite Gautreau, Rosemary Duncan, Joyce Kemp, Ann Wylder, Mary Peters, and Mary Jennings. Sister Barbara Ehrler, r.c., of the Lantana, Florida, Cenacle introduced Fr. David Fleming, SJ, to the value of the publication of this book. In turn, Fr. Fleming blessed our work with the gift of his opening words.

The Chicago Province of the Society of Jesus never wavered in their appreciation for Irene's formative role in many of their lives. Fr. Michael Cooper's friendship was a lifeline more than once.

Many in Irene's women's group offered their support to this project in countless ways, especially Marie Crosby, Monnie Lindsey, Sharron Traver Muzio, and Margaret Comella.

Professor Emeritus of English Rosemary Hake always found time to review correspondence, various versions of proposals, and offer insightful guidance.

Without the artful crafting of the well-said word by Chiron Publications editor Siobhan Drummond, this work would be less than the richly woven text it is. We are grateful to Susan Harris, who offered careful, final touches as the concluding project manager and editor, and to Peter Altenberg for his artistic cover and typesetting design.

Noreen Sullivan generously used her considerable skills in bibliographic research, Internet searches, and conversational support over the long haul of this first phase of the Dugan Legacy Project.

Mary Beth Kirchner, independent radio producer and national programming consultant, met Irene years ago and originally produced an audiotape for Irene's introduction to the book. Following Irene's death, Mary Beth graciously gave of her time and talent to produce the video that is included on the enhanced compact disc that accompanies this book. In turn, Mary Beth recommended Robin Wise, an independent audio engineer who creates compact disc masters and, as she says, "mixes anything that comes across her desk!" Robin directed me to Mary Gaffney of WBEZ radio in Chicago, who worked with me in producing the audio portion of the meditations. Robin's artistry with digital audio and DVD mastery engineered the creation of the enhanced CD. Such an undertaking was unimaginable to Irene; she would be so delighted to think of this high-tech addition to her book.

The beautiful improvised reflective piano music on the CD created by Jerri Greer, Ph.D., found its way into the Dugan project by a design larger than ourselves.

We are indebted to David Lafkas for the gift of his wise legal counsel.

Finally, let me speak in a singular voice. The dedication page that reads *pro omnibus sororibus misericordiae* is my dedication to "all sisters of mercy." I may never have met Sister Irene Dugan if not for my life as a Sister of Mercy. You are the waters of Jordan in which I was baptized into my desire for spiritual maturity. In a special way, the completion of this book is tied to your continuing sisterhood with me. It was Sister of Mercy Mary Ann Bergfeld, Irene's treasured friend in religious life, who first introduced me to Irene thirty-three years ago. Mary Ann has walked this way with me and knows my gratitude to her for her companionship and counsel.

I owe a huge debt of gratitude to Judith Bobber who has literally lived with me through the hills and valleys of the mystery and sometimes misery of carrying this book with me and in me through these years; she is a saint.

Lastly, let my final words here be spoken as the spiritual daughter of the voice. Hear my voice whispering from earth to heaven, "Irene, not only did you not miss the boat, but the wafting of your spirit is wind in my sails."

Epiphany 2004

Editor's Note

SISTER IRENE DUGAN RECOMMENDED THAT BEFORE BEGINNING THE exploration of your life journey as suggested in *Love Is All Around in Disguise*, you listen to and watch the accompanying enhanced compact disc to glean the "why" of the book. You will hear in her own voice her commitment to the "wedding of the art forms of spirituality and human experience." She calls us to realize the wisdom waiting to be culled from the experience of our own lives. The accompanying disc is meant to provide an enhancement to the work that awaits you as you travel through the text.

Sister Dugan suggests that you will maximize your benefit from this book by relying on five additional resources. The first is an edition of the Spiritual Exercises of St. Ignatius, such as *Draw Me into Your Friendship: A Literal Translation and Contemporary Reading of the Spiritual Exercises* (Fleming 1996), and the second is *At a Journal Workshop: Writing to Access the Power of the Unconscious and Evoke Creative Ability* by Ira Progoff (1992). These two men were significant influences on Irene Dugan's spiritual vision. She names them as experts at providing direction for those who are serious about life's journey to selfhood and union with God. More will be said about each of them later.

The third resource is the Bible, a book that never fades in memory. The Bible (meaning "book") has two main sections – the Old Testament or Hebrew Scriptures and the New Testament or Christian Scriptures. It is an enduring classic religious text that possesses a revelatory timelessness. The Hebrew and Christian Scriptures are a cornucopia of literature, history, geography, archeology, anthropology, linguistics, origins of religion, expressions of faith, song, myth, and symbol. For those who claim the Book as sacred, the Bible is an encounter with Incomprehensible Mystery and a source of enduring meaning about life and its purposes.

> *For the mystery of the text,*
> *and for the history of eyes to see*
> *and ears to hear the text,*
> *we give you thanks.*
>
> . . . .
>
> *We pray for the gift of perception.*
> *We pray for energy and courage,*
> *that we may not leave the text*
> *until we wrench your blessing from it.*
>
> —Walter Brueggemann
> (from Searcy 2003, p. 81)

While the issues of historical context, authorship, authenticity, verifiability, genre, audience, and a score of other questions are vitally important for scholarly exegesis, the purpose of its place in this book rests on the durability of the ancient text to incite memory and imagination within the context of current human experience. Our focus is not on critical scholarship or canonical hermeneutics as such, but on the dramatic portrayal of the old stories erupting again into a moment of contemporary personal consciousness. Ancient texts can be re-uttered and re-heard with new relevance and poignancy. The Bible discloses a God unintimidated by modernity, unimpressed by excessive religion, nondefensive about epistemology, daring to insist that the God of many guises in word and wonders is still at large in the world, liberating and healing (Brueggemann 2000, p. 39).

The fourth resource is a private journal or notebook to record your responses to the suggested guided exercises and meditations; it will assist you in deepening your experience of encounters with your own interior life. The act of "uncensored" writing bridges the inner and outer worlds in which we live. It creates an avenue of expression for the unconscious to emerge through the conscious activity of writing. There are only a few rules that govern journal writing: (1) your entries form a private document and belong exclusively to you; while you may choose to share your journal entries verbally with your spiritual mentor, no one should be given direct access to your writing; (2) the writing should flow freely without self-censure of any idea, thought, recollection, memory, or feeling; (3) date every entry that you make; and (4) don't make any other rules. (See Baldwin 1990 and track 3 of the CD for a fuller explanation of keeping a journal.) More specific instructions for various kinds of journal entries will be explained as you work through the exercises that are suggested in the following chapters.

Finally, a mentor or spiritual companion is an added advantage for engaging in the inner work recommended in this book. Irene Dugan believed we are given as a gift to one another, as fellow travelers on the journey. A spiritual mentor is a skilled and trustworthy companion who works with you to raise your level of consciousness regarding self-knowledge, assists in articulating what is happening in your interior realms, discerns the nature of obstacles obstructing your growth, and listens to and with you as you enter more deeply into your inner world and its workings.

While Sister Dugan recommends the above avenues of support to experience optimal benefit from this book, one can work with the text independent of any other resources.

... *statements made in the Holy Scriptures are also utterances of the soul . . . .*

—C. G. Jung
(from *Answer to Job*, par. 557)

I thought at first [the Bible] was an arid book. But then I found it wise and a bit – merry.

—the character of Emily Dickinson in *The Belle of Amherst* (Luce 1976, p. 27)

I write these pages not for the learned or academic but for the seekers, flounderers, stargazers, and lovers, such as myself.

Irene Dugan, r.c.
May 1997

1. Introduction

⚜

MY FRIENDS, FOLKS IN CLASS, AND OTHERS ALONG THE WAY have been after me for years to write a book. They keep saying, "Irene, you can't die unless you leave something for us." I couldn't understand why this seemed so important to them. I figured if I were giving them anything permanent surely it was the giving of myself every single day. In spite of this objection, the word kept coming, "Write a book! Write a book!" About ten years ago, I started to write about Ignatius of Loyola (1491–1556) and Ira Progoff (1921–1998), two men who are very important to me.[1] My first writing effort was an attempt to integrate their ideas and teachings for the contemporary spiritual seeker; this attempt failed for various reasons.

After a period of dormancy and under creative pressure of students and friends, I forged ahead into the work you are now reading. While separated by five centuries, the insights and interior growth skills developed by Ignatius of Loyola and Ira Progoff are vitally important for those in the twenty-first century who are serious about engaging the depths of spirituality. But before proceeding further, it is important to have a sense of the vision, inventiveness, and spiritual daring of Ignatius and Progoff.

Ignatius of Loyola

Ignatius, a Spaniard of the sixteenth century, was born in 1491 to a wealthy family from a Basque province. He was the youngest son of thirteen children and by age sixteen was involved in the affairs of his world. Ignatius became a courtier, fond of gambling, swordplay, and the chivalrous world of knighthood. He dreamt all the dreams of the gallantry of his times. He was going to do marvelous things for the "princesses" without reckoning God's intervention and God's designs. From one of his own letters he tells us that he was "a man given to the follies of the world . . . with a great and foolish desire to win fame." He was also particularly careless about his affairs with women (Rahner 1960, p. 8).

In 1521, an officer at thirty years of age, he was defending the fortress of the town of Pamplona against the French who claimed the territory as their own against Spain. The commander of the Spanish forces urged surrender in the face of the far mightier French forces. Ignatius convinced him to fight, even to defeat, for the honor of Spain. During this battle, Ignatius was seriously wounded in both legs. He was forced to convalesce in the castle of Loyola, where he underwent several operations without anesthetic to repair his serious and disfiguring wounds. It was an injury from which he never fully recovered. Like the biblical Jacob, Ignatius walked with a limp for the rest of his life. And, like Jacob, it was a sacred wound which changed the course of his life.

His lengthy recuperation forced the active nobleman and warrior Ignatius to rest and reflect. The only books available in the castle were a four-volume life of Christ and the lives of the saints. Serious reading was new to Ignatius, and with it he experienced a journey into previously unexplored regions of his interior life. This was the beginning of his religious conversion and discovery of spiritual discernment, or discernment of spirits, which is at the heart of his Spiritual Exercises.

The drama of his conversion led Ignatius to abandon his old desires for conquest, romance, and worldly power. Recovered from his wounds, though limping, Ignatius decided to make a pilgrimage to Jerusalem to walk the way Jesus walked. Leaving behind knife, sword, and fine clothes, Ignatius began a new way of life not knowing where it would lead.

His journey took him toward Barcelona, the point of embarkation for Rome, where pilgrims sought permission to visit the Holy Land. Ignatius stopped first, however, in Manressa where he stayed in a cave outside of the town. While intending to stay only a short time, Ignatius was drawn into the deeper caverns of his own interior life. He experienced an encounter with God – a vision – that would direct him to embrace the truth that life is the journey of "finding God in all things." This grace, finding God in all things, remains a core virtue of Jesuit spirituality. It was in the literal and metaphorical cave at Manressa that Ignatius began to detail his own experience of spiritual awakening and conversion, and he drew on these in articulating the Spiritual Exercises that became the heart of Ignatian spirituality and mission.

Ignatius composed and revised the Spiritual Exercises over a twenty-five-year period prior to their publication in 1548. The Spiritual Exercises of St. Ignatius contain instructions, admonitions, annotations, examinations, warnings, methods, prayers, meditations, and other "exercises" designed to lead one to virtue, discernment of spirits, renewal in faith, assertion of direction in life, and psychospiritual transformation through love.

After completing his pilgrimage to the Holy Land, Ignatius set his mind to a serious study of theology and philosophy. He continued to share his insights with those who were open to experiencing the ways of spiritual growth he directed. Twice he was investigated by the Spanish Inquisition and even imprisoned for a time. He eventually made his way to the University of Paris where he met Francis Xavier and Peter Faber. Under the influence of Ignatius's Spiritual Exercises, they were drawn into Ignatius's vision and eventually assisted him in founding the Society of Jesus.

In 1537, at the age of forty-five, Ignatius was ordained a priest. Two years later, the Society of Jesus was founded. Ignatius and his two companions decided to go to Rome and place themselves at the disposal of the pope. Pope Paul III approved the formation of the *Societas Jesu* in 1540 and the wounded warrior mystic Ignatius watched his small company grow to a thousand members before his death in 1556. (See "A Biography of Ignatius Loyola" by Rev. Norman O'Neal, SJ [2000], and "Chivalry Inspired a Courtier Saint" by Margot Patterson [2001].)

Although physically a small man, Ignatius possessed immense spiritual strength once he opened himself to the divine healing (wholeness) emanating from his experience of being wounded. His

Spiritual Exercises are what are important now. They have an ever-present freshness, touching the spirit as the morning dew. Nearly four and a half centuries later, his insights remain vital and viable for the spiritual seeker on the pilgrimage of life. His work leads us to exercise the inner-world muscles of intellect, will, memory, imagination, and interior senses, thus allowing us to encounter and explore our own yearning for identity, meaning, purpose, and destiny in living the gift of our lifetime.

Ignatius and his companions were keenly aware that those on the spiritual quest need guides to traverse the spiritual paths. Without help, the searchers are left floundering and often in the dark for far too long. Ignatius's dream was to have men and women who themselves are searchers to walk and talk with the floundering and the lost. Thus, the permanently meaningful insights of Ignatian spirituality have influenced countless people who desire to walk the way of spiritual consciousness suggested in these pages.

Ira Progoff

Ira Progoff, a holistic depth psychologist, was born in 1921 and devoted his life to the exploration of new ways to encourage creativity and to enhance personal and spiritual growth. Ira Progoff studied with the father of modern depth psychology, Carl Gustav Jung, in the early 1950s. Progoff's clinical practice and research on the dynamic process whereby people develop fulfilling lives led him to pioneer the field known as *holistic* depth psychology. Similar to Ignatian spirituality, holistic depth psychology aims to assist individuals to develop more fully by exercising their interior capacities to examine their lived experience and make choices about the quality and direction of their lives.

Progoff believed that reentering the transitions of life and reflecting on the dynamics of change in one's lived experience helps build a sensitivity to the inner rhythms of change. Reconstructing one's own life path, including obstacles and roads taken and not taken, enlarges interior perspectives on experience and reveals patterns of choice. Through this inner process creative integrations can take place. Holistic depth psychology takes into consideration the whole of one's lived experience, not presumed to be ladened with pathology. Pathology is caused by a departure from our natural orientation toward growth, a rupture in our becoming. Pathology arises from the blocking of the flow of creative energy. When our potentials are stymied, we become sick. In holistic depth psychology, the individual is not a "case" history, but rather possesses a "life" history. Progoff's *Intensive Journal®* method provides a framework for positioning the individual between past and future, placing his or her life in context and perspective, and enabling the person to make life-giving decisions in a self-reliant and healing way.[2]

Progoff's holistic depth psychology, Jung's theories, and the Christian theological and spiritual tradition espoused by Ignatius merge in the conviction that planted deep within each person is a drive toward wholeness – the ultimate integration of self with Transcendent Center, God.

Progoff employs the notion of soul from a Jungian perspective – with deep-rooted realization that the soul is the power of all human life. It is important to grasp this in order to appreciate our own power to cultivate the rich territory of the *psyche*, a Greek word for "soul." Jung's notions of *anima* and *animus* are key to unlocking his understanding of the soul as part of psychic structure. Jung does not refer to the soul in a traditional religious way. *Anima* means "soul" in Latin, and *animus* means "spirit." From a certain psychological point of view, there is no difference in meaning between the two Latin terms. If one thinks of the soul (*anima*) as leaving the body at the time of death, it is the same as saying that a person's spirit (*animus*) has departed. In the Christian tradition, based on the faith of ancient Israel, the Spirit or *Shekkinah* of God is often depicted as wind, breath, or air, and there is always a last breath within the body that, from a religious point of view, wafts the spirit of the person from this life to the next. Thus, the terms are used interchangeably, and most importantly, both words refer to the inner world of human beings, to the soulful and spiritual dimensions of human existence. (See Murray Stein, *Practicing Wholeness* [1996, pp. 91–94] and *Jung's Map of the Soul,* chapter 6, "The Way to the Deep Interior" [1998, pp. 125–149]. *Ed.*)

The Progoff life-study method is a mode of relationship rather than a mode of analysis. It is interesting to me that Progoff points out that everything a person does or becomes is of value. As a psychotherapist, he found that his clients who wrote in some form of a journal were able to work through issues and painful obstacles in their lives more rapidly and with greater satisfaction. Through his research, he developed and refined the *Intensive Journal*® method in the mid-1960s and 1970s. *At a Journal Workshop* (1992) is the text that articulates both his theories of personal/spiritual growth and the methods or processes by which people become inwardly attuned and discover the hidden potential to develop themselves.

My years of working with him and others in using his *Intensive Journal*® method prove to me the importance of this tool for self-development and interior vitality. He is the most nonjudgmental person I have ever met; he made everyone, including myself, feel special. What better approach helps a person believe in himself or herself? Progoff knew that the soul only speaks its truth in an atmosphere of quiet, empathy, invitation, and trust.

Progoff, like Ignatius, is very insistent that "inner movements," which are always going on inside the human being – thinking, writing, planning scenarios, the interior or intrapersonal dialoguing – be given attention. This inner activity can be disorganized, undirected, at times wasteful and destructive. The Ignatian Exercises integrated with insights from Ira Progoff can help to make inner work intentional, productive, and self-directed.

Ignatius could have been a twentieth-century holistic depth psychologist and Progoff a sixteenth-century spiritual visionary.

—Irene Dugan, r.c.

The exercises of holistic depth psychology and of spirituality – the wedding of the art forms of spirituality and life experience – help us discern the workings of destructive and creative forces busy within us. The narrative that unfolds from this conscious engagement is the story of human becoming, a story of accepting limitations on one hand and of realizing potentials hidden in disguise on the other. Attending to psychospiritual insights and methods can lead to enlightenment and transformation.

Making a Journal Entry

Both Ignatius and Progoff believed that the truth we are seeking is waiting within ourselves for discovery. As Sanford has noted, "The rediscovery of the personal and creative side of Christianity is more possible today than it has been for many centuries, because of the uncovering of the unconscious. The discovery of the reality of the inner world – of which we are ordinarily unaware, but which greatly affects our conscious life – is the most important religious fact of our time and adds a great impetus to our search for an inner Christianity" (Sanford 1987, pp. 9–10). Deeper self-knowledge and interior growth will not be found in reading a book but in doing one's own emotional and spiritual homework. Just as you can't get in shape by reading a book on exercise, so you will not experience greater inner attunement without exercising the interior muscles of the inner world outlined in this book. Thus, the whole of this book is an exercise in practical spirituality.

To begin to get a feel for the process, try the following exercise. You may also choose to listen to tracks 4 and 5 on the CD.

1. Create for yourself an atmosphere of stillness. You may want to read from the Hebrew Scriptures, Psalm 46:10, "Be still and know that I am God," or from the Book of Sirach 2:3, "Cling to God and never let go." Gaze at this verse and repeat the phrase until you sense its invitation. An atmosphere of outer and inner stillness supports the entry into interior realms.

2. Make a decision to honor what emerges from your depths and give yourself permission to allow the words to flow without any filtering or judgment.

3. Listen with interior ears to the following questions. As words, thoughts, or feelings begin to arise, in language or other symbolic form, record them in your journal. Date your entry.

4. Begin your journey within by paying attention to the words or phrases or images that surface that characterize you. Your central question is, Who am I? Combine it with the questions, How well do I know myself? Who has influenced or imbalanced this image of myself? How much have I authored my life or have I handed over my power to others? What is the vision of myself that I carry within?

These are awe-filled considerations: if we are alive, we do not want to be identified by a job, a role, a position, a profession, or by some function we perform. Each of us is an individual, especially gifted and different. The answers to the fundamental questions, Who am I? and Where am I going? are seeded within us. We can resolve the question, Is the life that I am living the same life that wants to live in me? (Palmer 2000, p. 2).

> *I shall stand at my post,*
> *I shall station myself on my watch-tower,*
> *watching to see what God will say to me,*
> *what answer, God will make to my complaints.*
> *Then God answered me and said,*
> *"Write the vision down,*
> *inscribe it on tablets*
> *to be easily read.*
>
> *For the vision will have its appointed time,*
> *it hastens towards its end and it will not lie;*
> *although it may take some time, wait for it,*
> *for come it certainly will before too long."*
>
> The Book of Habakkuk 2:1–3 (NJB)

Notes

1. Dates have been added, as Dr. Ira Progoff died in 1998, one year after Irene Dugan. *Ed.*

2. For more detail on Progoff's *Intensive Journal*® method see Joyce Kemp, r.c, in "The Discernment of Life Tasks in the Progoff *Intensive Journal*® Process" in *Spirituality in Depth* (Clendenen 2002, pp. 69–80). Sister Kemp is a certified Progoff *Intensive Journal*® consultant leading workshops and seminars at the Cenacle Retreat House and Spirituality Center in Warrenville, Illinois. For more information, contact the Center at (800) 240-6702 or visit their Web site at www.cenacle.org.

2. The Artistry and Awe of Creation

⁂

A CLASSIC WORK IN CHRISTIAN SPIRITUALITY, THE SPIRITUAL Exercises of St. Ignatius are often practiced in their original form in the context of a thirty-day retreat. A retreat of this length boggles the mind of many who cannot imagine devoting so much time to interior travel. While we may lust for the luxuries of a month-long vacation, planning and saving for such an opportunity, we would rarely think of doing what Ignatius came to believe was essential to the experience of abundant living. The thirty-day retreat calls for the spiritual seeker to spend five hours each day in prayer. The Spiritual Exercises are divided into four themes, each one week long. Since we live in linear time, the Exercises are laid out to accommodate the usual way we live our lives. Hours, days, and weeks demarcate the movement through the Exercises. It is important to note, however, that chronological time does not govern growth in the context of the spiritual journey. God's grace will work within the human senses and soul in such a way as to "move" the person in terms of *kairos*, a Greek word for entry into sacred time.

Ignatius launches the Spiritual Exercises with a consideration he names the "Principle and Foundation," which is one of the bookends holding the whole of the Book of Ignatian Exercises together. God's creativity, the gift of life and love coupled with the realization of the great Genesis myth telling the story of human failure and radical limitation, mark the themes of the first week. Week two explores the story of Jesus and his life works. The focus of week three embraces the reality of human suffering as revealed through the passion of Jesus. Week four celebrates the joy in finding life even in death or, said another way, a reflection on the Resurrection. The other bookend of the Exercises is known as "Contemplations on the Universal Love" we yearn to obtain. Love is the girdle of strength binding the work of the Exercises together, a web of threads which though slender are strong. Robert Johnson gives meaning to the magnificent and mysterious threads that weave through our lives when he asks and answers the question:

> What are these threads? Being in a particular place at just the right time, meeting someone who steers you in an unforeseen direction, the unexpected appearance of work or money or inspiration just when they are most needed. These are the mysterious forces that guide us and shape who we are. They are the patterns that give meaning to our experience. (Johnson 1998, p. xi).

> *She who reconciles the ill-matched threads*
> *of her life, and weaves them gratefully*
> *into a single cloth—*
> . . . .
> *With each disclosure you encompass more*
> *and she stretches beyond what limits her, to hold you.*
>
> —Rainer Maria Rilke, "Wer seines Lebens viele Widersinne"
> (from *Rilke's Book of Hours: Love Poems to God*, p. 64)

Ignatius, in his wisdom, knew even in the sixteenth century that people couldn't often separate from the demands of their ordinary lives to engage in the extraordinary experience of a thirty-day retreat. Therefore, his Exercises include an accommodation or annotation that stretches these themes over a lengthier period of time. The 19th Annotation permits individuals to embrace the Exercises in the midst of *en vie courant*, in our running or busy lives.[1]

However one encounters the Exercises, the seeker will discover that Ignatius's concern was that those in search of the examined life could develop the spiritual art form of contemplation – praying or centering the soul by using the uniquely human faculties of our senses and imagination. Ignatius directed his spiritual disciples to pay attention to their innermost desires, the movements of consolation and contentment, as well as the movements of desolation and discontent. Ignatian spirituality is an intuitive spirituality that holds as fundamentally trustworthy the affective or emotional dimension of our lives. Ignatius presses the serious spiritual seeker to go beyond mental prayer or recitation of prayers to explore the deeper dynamics inside one's own inner world.

Ignatius relies on the stories of Jesus found in the Christian scriptures in order for spiritual seekers to free their imaginations to contemplate and place themselves in the scenes of Jesus' life. Why? Ignatius discovered that in confronting his own wounds by contemplating the gospel stories of Jesus he somehow reconnected to a larger story of an enduring truth that provided him a newfound sense of healing and hope.

Many of us seem to need a deep wounding or profound loss before we wake up, or experience what we call spiritual awakening, an altering of consciousness from which we can never be the same again. This is a definition of spiritual conversion. Once Ignatius discovered his sacred core, even though never fully recovered from his physical wound, he became energized with purpose and direction in life. Thus, contemplation of sacred stories, even by those who do not share the Christian faith, assist our postmodern selves – separate, fragmented, and isolated – in reconnecting with the deeper layers of experience we share with humanity, the whole culture, and with all creation. Jung called this the collective unconscious, a source of universal wisdom, guidance, and ultimate meaning. Even when we feel most separate and different from others, it is important to remember that our common psychological home – the psyche/soul – remains the same.

Ignatius's spiritual intent of "finding God in all things" includes our experience of fallenness and finitude and is in harmony with the holistic depth psychology of Progoff. Each person is made to be a reflection and image of God's own creativity. There is Divine Intentionality seeded deep with each individual. The Divine lures us in the direction of our most radiant self. We will turn our

attention to the intersection of Progoff with Ignatius following a
more detailed foray into Ignatius's "Principle and Foundation."

. . . in the beginning

The first week of the Exercises of St. Ignatius is a historical journey
through time, looking at how we are loved and how we turn away
from love. Since the Christian scriptures bear witness to the conviction that God is love, we can use the word *love* to mean God.
Ignatius stresses that Love is an expression of the pouring out of life
in abundance through the inexhaustible wonder of creation. Love
created and formed the first humans, placed them in a mythic garden with all they needed to be and who they were shaped to be.
Sovereignty was theirs over this varied and vivid expression of
overflowing life. A journey began out of this outpouring of life and
Love, flowing a day at a time to the point of the full fruition of each
expression of life.

We are invited by Ignatius in the Exercise called "Principle and
Foundation" to enter into the dynamism of creation in order to place
ourselves in the center of this awesome act of Love. The garden
described in the Hebrew Scripture's Book of Genesis (2:1–24) was a
world in itself, set up in such a way as to assure the continuation of
each species of life. The Creator and creative God of Genesis, chapter
1, is referred to in the plural: "Then God said, let *us* make humankind
in *our* image, after *our* likeness" (Gen. 1:26 NRSV, italics mine). As
master crafters, they drafted plans and watched them explode in creation like an artist in wild colorful creativity on canvas. Imagine what
they must have felt, what they planned and hoped would happen?
Their whole Being was expressed and invested in this work wrought
out of loving wisdom.

Marvel of marvels, each species had within itself a shared Divine
power to pass on life. In the stories of Genesis 1 and 2, the precious-
ness of life is superbly underlined, as is the power vested in humans.
A'dam, the earth creature, was called by God to name each animal
(Genesis 2:18–20), to be partner with earth, ocean, and Divine Love.
Harmony of the spheres prevailed; it is a picture beyond our imag-
ing precisely because of its magnitude and magnificence.

Pondering this beginning, called creation by some or by some the "Big Bang," one finds the word *name* electrified. The Divine had everything named specially. Each member of one species is unique just like the unmatched intricacy of a set of individual fingerprints or the unique stripes on each and every zebra. Wonder of wonders, naming every aspect of the created universe with such artistry and thus giving meaning and purpose to each individual creature within the domain of the created universe.

There is abundance in every species and aspect of creation. The mythic truth is that we need not yearn or plead for Love since it is all around us in the disguise of creation itself. The poet Hopkins captured this artistry in these words:

> *The world is charged with the grandeur of God,*
> *It will flame out, like shining from shook foil;*
> *It gathers to greatness, like the ooze of oil*
> *Crushed. Why do men then now not reck his rod?*
> *Generations have trod, have trod, have trod;*
> *And all is seared with trade; bleared, smeared with toil;*
> *And wears man's smudge and shares man's smell: the soil*
> *Is bare now, nor can foot feel, being shod.*
>
> *And for all this, nature is never spent;*
> *There lives the dearest freshness deep down things;*
> *And though the last lights off the black West went*
> *Oh, morning, at the brown brink eastward, springs—*
> *Because the Holy Ghost over the bent*
> *World broods with warm breast and with ah!*
> *bright wings.*
>
> —Gerard M. Hopkins, "God's Grandeur" (1952, p. 70)

The Garden and the Cosmos of Our Becoming

Together, the Exercises of Ignatius and Progoff's insights into our interior processes place us in the immediacy of the metaphorical garden and simultaneously at the center of the cosmos, so that we can look out at our environment and find our place. Formidable and vast, the cosmos is nonetheless composed of the smallest and largest images of our Maker. The tiniest ant and the towering mountains evoke images of infinite care and limitless grandeur. No wonder the question of identity looms so large in society. We long to know about ourselves, our roots, and all the whys and wherefores. Here the intersection with Progoff's insights suggests that the journey to self-knowledge *is* the journey into God.

Progoff's starting place of self-knowledge is a microcosm of the major work of the cosmos, none other than that of each individual self. What better place to begin than with the now? God's creativity began with the self-expression of creation. As part of that creative act of Love, in the birth of unique names, we begin deeper contemplation by situating ourselves at the point where our lives are presently.

Putting Ignatius's and Progoff's tools together can help anyone who wishes to enter the process toward wholeness or holiness. The process is rigorous, freeing, and rewarding, all in one. It is an awesome process, full of ups and downs, light and darkness, clarity and mystery, serenity and risk-taking.

The objective is to free us gradually to be unafraid to look at the experiences of our life so as to learn from our lived experience and then to modify or to enhance our behavior, our inner environment, and our life goals. The material and methods in this book are aids to attain spiritual freedom, the power to act – not out of social pressure or personal fear, but from the deep core of one's being – where Love beckons to our fullest radiant becoming.

Meditation Focus and Processes

You are invited to begin a meditation period that will first take seriously the divine creative God-life that has been breathed deeply into you. You were given life, fashioned in God's image, and also given the divine impulse to cherish, nurture, and steward the creation given into human care. The focus of the meditation will then move to an examination requiring sufficient self-critical honesty to look at how you have misused and sometimes rejected the gift of life.

The Importance of Desire

Before beginning the period of meditation it is important to reflect on a common concern shared by both Ignatius and Progoff. Although separated by centuries of chronological time, both men encouraged serious students of the inner quest to grow in their awareness of the importance of the human capacity for desire. Synonyms for *desire* include *wish, yearn, hunger, hanker,* and *longing.* We are conceived and born enwrapped in desire. We come forth from the womb wrapped in the need for food, warmth, help, shelter, touch, security, and love. Our deepest desire is to live; our physicality, our psyche, and our spirituality give witness to this truth about human nature.

Ignatius's biography reveals him as a man of great and intense desires. At the time of his conversion he indulged in an exercise that Progoff best described as "holy daydreaming." The man of action had to give in to a lengthy healing process of wasting time resting, reading, and reflecting. While in a resting mode, he would see himself in fantasy undertaking great things for God. By use of imagination Ignatius placed himself in scenes with Christ and enacted the lives of the saints. Remember, these were the only books available to him in the castle at Loyola. He tells us that this holy exercise always left him with a feeling of peace, devotion, and strength that he later termed *spiritual consolation.*

Progoff refers to a similar state as "twilight dreaming." In preparing to enter a deeper state of consciousness, Progoff urges the seeker to enter the stream of an interior process perceived on the screen of the mind's eye. We allow images, feelings, and actions to emerge within the state suspended between wakefulness and actual dreaming. He says, "We do not guide it. We do not direct it. We do not restrict it. We encourage it to move on its own and in its own way wherever it wishes to go" (1992, pp. 207–208).

This makes good psychological sense. You can hardly achieve what you cannot even see in imagination. You must be a person of great desires and great vision if you are going to be mighty in achievement. In a world in which we give so much importance to achievement, we are apt to overlook the tremendous value of desire as a guiding light for authentic achievement.

*Enter by the narrow gate; for the gate is wide
and the road easy that leads to destruction, and there
are many who take it. For the gate is narrow and the
road is hard that leads to life, and there are few who find it.*

—Matthew 7:13–14 (NRSV)

And because the way *and path* is difficult and the gate *through which one passes and enters* to life is narrow, there are both few who *walk it and enter through* it.

And if there are some who walk that way for a while, there are very few who persevere on it.

But how blessed are those to whom it has been given to walk *that way and* to persevere till the end.

—St. Clare of Assisi (1194–1253 C.E.)
(from *Clare of Assisi: Early Documents*, p. 59)

Implanted within the human being is a drive to live fully and to work at living. Unfortunately, "to live fully" and "to work at living" are often at odds. To live fully and to work at it requires a study of life, its needs, its demands, its purpose, and its end. One lives in the tension of the pulls of opposites. One is drawn in the direction of the biblical "narrow gate and hard road" leading to life and, simultaneously, in the direction of the "wide gate and easy road" of self-destruction (Mt. 7:13).

Theologically, it is imperative that we explore "in the beginning" where God's desires for God's own handiwork are made manifest. It is the imagination of the Trinity – the three-in-oneness of God – that is the divine energy that begets the dynamic of love and life. Their imagination, mind, and will, propelled by love, imaged us. Our entry into the mystery of the Trinity suggests that only those who permit the symbolic to operate can grasp why images are so important. The holy daydreaming of Ignatius and the twilight imagining of Progoff provoke the awakening of the symbol-maker in us. (See Margaret Zulaski, OSF, in "Dreams – Hidden Treasures of the Unconsciousness" (Clendenen 2002, pp. 35–45) for a discussion of the symbolic importance of dreams.) In *The Bonding of Will and Desire*, Stroud reminds us:

> Desire is closely allied with *Eros*. Our hearts' desire is for Life, Light, and Love, a longing for union for intimacy. There is a still more inward interplay in desire between desire and fear: we fear what we desire and we desire what we fear; we see dread in the shadow of fascination and fascination in the shadow of dread.

> Before any act, we need to say to ourselves, in the silence of our being, what is it we *will* to become; we need to convince ourselves of our own becoming and to exalt it for ourselves. (1994, p. 180)

The work is not to be just in the head or the heart, but with every part of oneself so as to make possible bringing one's whole self into the experience of one's own becoming.

Read the following suggestions for meditation and choose one process in order to prepare to enter more deeply into the focus of the meditation that is outlined in this section.

Prelude

1. Create for yourself an atmosphere of stillness. Give yourself permission to cross over from linear or chronological time into *kairos*, sacred time. You may want to select a favorite biblical verse. Gaze at the verse and repeat the phrase until you sense that you are entering into its invitation. An atmosphere of outer and inner stillness supports the entry into the interior realms.

2. Make a decision to honor what emerges from your depths and give yourself permission to allow what emerges to flow without any filtering and judgment.

3. Listen with interior ears to your responses to the questions Ignatius recommends addressing as one enters into a period of deep reflection: What am I about to do? With whom will I be meeting? What am I seeking? As words, thoughts, feelings begin to arise in language or symbol, record them in your journal. Date your entry.

A Progoff *Entrance Meditation*™

Another approach to preparing for meditation is the preparatory ritual Progoff refers to as an "*Entrance Meditation*™." Your goal is to enter into the quiet inner space of your being.

1. Sit quietly, let your shoulders drop, plant both feet flat on the floor, uncross your arms to be free for deep breathing.

2. Be aware of thoughts, noises, or body sensations demanding attention. Be aware of them and then let them go.

3. Be aware of any persons in the same place with you. Be intensively aware and then let them go.

4. Slowly read and fall into the flow of Progoff's *Entrance Meditation*™ entitled "Letting the Self Become Still":

> *Letting the Self become still,*
> *Letting our thoughts come to rest,*
> *Letting our breath become slow.*
> *Breathing becomes quiet,*
> *Breathing becomes slow,*
> *And slower;*
> *Breathing becomes regular,*
> *Regular.*
> *The unevenness*
> *Of nonessential thoughts*
> *Drops out of the breathing.*

It becomes
The breathing of the Self.
(Progoff 1971, p. 39)

5. Take your time entering this quieting exercise before jump-ing into meditation. This exercise is meant to be an effort-less transition into meditation.

6. Make a decision to honor what emerges from your depths and give yourself permission to allow what emerges to flow without any filtering and judgment. As words, thoughts, feelings begin to arise in language or symbol, record them in your journal. Date your entry.

Since graceful and fluid body movement aids inner quiet and sharp awareness, you may want to consider experimenting with some bodywork as part of your process to deeper meditation. Don't be intimidated by using your body in gestures that present themselves to you, such as opening your hands to bodily enjoin the desire for greater openness. Tai chi and aikido are excellent modes of grace in movement, neither violent nor straining but full of beauty. Prayer time is approached with more ease and readiness when the body is relaxed. Body movement that rises in you at any time is appropriate and expressive of whom you are and long to be.

A good way to enter this time is to bring your whole being into the experience. Thus, each time of meditation begins with a prayer of awareness of this special time set aside to be in communion with God. We have to begin by calming our inner space, acknowledging what we are about is of primary importance because we are placing before God what we desire. The desire flows from the subject or primary focus of the meditation.

Deeper Meditation or Contemplation

Now place before God the desires you have for yourself. Expose your innermost yearnings about all the great things you desire to be and do. The fact that you will never actually do them or that you feel incapable of doing them is irrelevant. What is important is that you *experience desire*. You allow yourself to reveal to God how immense your desires are even though your strength or capacity to actualize them is limited. It is thus that lovers speak when they express the immensity of desires that far outdistance their limited capacity.

Make those great deeds your own through desiring them, willing them, even performing them in fantasy, which is a form of Ignatian contemplation. Fantasize that you yourself, by God's grace, are doing exactly what you perceive in your holy daydreaming. Give vent in fantasy to the ardent desires that your actual or perceived limitations or fears will not allow you to fulfill in reality.

A Journal Entry

Listen into the silence as the awesome word, memory, image, symbol, or gesture reveals itself. What arises is the blessing that wishes to wrench itself free from your unconscious. Trust recording it in your journal. Experience the contours of your own authentic desires. Date your entry.

Contemplation on the Divine Spark Hiding and Residing Within

As we gaze out at creation and inward on the amazing gift of life, Pierre Teilhard de Chardin's *Mass on the World* comes singing up from the depth of our being.

Creation sings with color, music, art, harmony, and beauty. The mountains in their somber solidity house every variety of life: roaring water falls, rippling creeks and brooks, animals, birds, fish, flowers of every color, and all kinds of species tended only by the Divine Gardener. Humans are custodians and guardians of all this array of the splendor of the Divine. The morning glory blooms fully for a day, the rose for a few more days; each revealing beauty of line, fragrance, color, and being itself.

The Offering

Since once again, Lord – though this time not in the forests of the Aisne but in the steppes of Asia – I have neither bread, nor wine, nor altar, I will raise myself beyond these symbols, up to the pure majesty of the real itself; I, your priest, will make the whole earth my altar and on it will offer you all the labours and sufferings of the world.

Over there, on the horizon, the sun has just touched with light the out-ermost fringe of the eastern sky. Once again, beneath this moving sheet of fire, the living surface of the earth wakes and trembles, and once again begins its fearful travail. I will place on my paten, O God, the harvest to be won by this renewal of labour. Into my chalice I shall pour all the sap, which is to be pressed out this day from the earth's fruits.

My paten and my chalice are the depths of a soul laid widely open to all the forces which in a moment will rise up from every corner of the earth and converge upon the Spirit. Grant me the remembrance and the mystic presence of all those whom the light is now awakening to the new day.

One by one, Lord, I see and I love all those whom you have given me to sustain and charm my life. One by one also I number all those who make up that other beloved family which has gradually surrounded me . . . I call before me the whole vast anonymous army of living humanity; those who surround me and support me though I do not know them; those who come, and those who go; above all, those who in office, school, laboratory and factory, through their vision of truth or despite their error, truly believe in the progress of earthly reality and who today will take up again their impassioned pursuit of the light.

This restless multitude, confused or orderly, the immensity of which ter-rifies us; this ocean of humanity whose slow, monotonous wave-flows trou-ble the hearts even of those whose faith is most firm: it is to this deep that I thus desire all the fibres of my being should respond. All the things in the world to which this day will bring increase; all those that will diminish; all those too that will die: all of them, Lord, I try to gather into my arms, so as to hold them out to you in offering. This is the material of my sacrifice; the only material you desire.

. . . .

Receive, O Lord, this all-embracing host that your whole creation, moved by your magnetism, offers you at this dawn of a new day.

This bread, our toil, is of itself, I know, but an immense fragmentation; this wine, our pain, is no more, I know, than a draught that dissolves . . . I yet have received from you an overwhelming sympathy for all that stirs within the dark mass of matter; because I know myself to be irremediably less a child of heaven than a child of earth; therefore I will this morning climb up in spirit to the high places, bearing with me the hopes and the miseries of my mother; and there – empowered by that priesthood which you alone (as I firmly believe) have bestowed on me – upon all that in the world of human flesh is now about to be born or to die beneath the rising sun I will call down the Fire.

. . . .

Over every living thing which is to spring up, to grow, to flower, to ripen during this day say again the words: This is my Body. And over every death-force which waits in readiness to corrode, to wither, to cut down, speak again your commanding words which express the supreme mystery of faith: This is my Blood.

—Teilhard de Chardin, *Hymn of the Universe* (1961, pp. 19–21, 23)

Each species of life contains a feminine and masculine aspect, as does God. There is no isolation in creation. We are all in it together, needing each other, relying on each other. The lion roars and waits in a listening mode for the answer of a mate, the wolf howls, the cardinal sings then listens. It is life calling on life. Like us, creation waits to be heard and answered. All that is required of this great astounding abundance of life are our reverent acts of attending.

All this glory is given to us that we can desire to learn the art form of praise and reverence. We, finite humans, viewing this panorama must swell with the desire for the infinite planted deep in us. There is the call of the world in all this. We possess the graced capacity for the willingness, the desire, to risk all in order to finish our work of cultivating all of life, especially our own.

God has made us for Godself because God is the beginning and end of all life. God wants us to respond to the call of life seeded deep within us. The Divine Energy is available at all times to augment our weakness in the face of all the lures and temptations that surround us on all sides. We were made by Love and given as well everything we need to respond in kind to Love; this is what we mean by grace. Grace is the spark of God-life always and everyday available to us to help us experience life as the gift that it is.

We must be immersed in our humanness, knowing that the less human we are the less redemptive we will be for ourselves as well as others. Far too many people live with only a passing acquaintance with their humanity.

Looking at our humanness with genuine interest plunges us into the fact that decisions about how we relate to the gift of life are an everyday matter-of-fact reality. On a daily basis we are making decisions either for life or against life. There is nothing neutral about our responsibility for self-creation. Because of freedom, our responses to this love gift can be one of receptivity or rejection.

> *I call heaven and earth to witness against you this day, that I have set before you life and death, blessings and curses. Choose life so that you and your descendants may live, loving the Lord your God, obeying God's voice, and cleaving to God; for that means life to you and length of days...*
>
> —Deuteronomy 30:19–20 (NRSV)

Rejecting the Gift

So much of the pain, sickness, violence, and death that marks and mars human culture are by-products of our misuse of freedom by rejecting our responsibility to develop our natural orientation to wholeness and holiness. The great Genesis myth of creation also includes the story of the Fall. This myth of origins tells us that human freedom introduced a tragic flaw, an original sin that distorts our true nature. Thus, our inclination to selfishness and domination disconnects us from our deeper desires for reciprocal tenderness, trust, community, harmony, and hope.

We are prone to suffer from a lack of security. Maybe ambiguity and anxiety are words that more accurately capture our struggle with human existence. Nothing is certain. No one can be counted on. Security means having a safe nest in money, position, family, and material things that will buffer us from the challenge of mutuality and interdependence of our deeper natures. False security disappoints over and over again.

> *The awareness of the ambiguity of one's highest achievements (as well as one's deepest failures) is a definite symptom of maturity.*
>
> —Paul Tillich (1886–1965)

Valid security comes with abiding and residing in the faith that we will be given what we need to make the journey called life. It takes strong love to live in such a way. Very often we do not and have not experienced strong love, which means we have been sinned against and, in turn, learned to sin. Such a state of affairs breeds hate, revenge, resistance to good, and overall unhappiness.

Our finitude – the finality of life we call death – is a major concern for us. The search for eternal youth is more intense than ever. Millions of dollars are spent each year on plastic surgery and liposuction, to name just two of many routes. Meanwhile, any true appreciation of the meaning of the passing of time is dismissed and suppressed in consciousness. Entry into aging is feared and denied by any artifice possible.

These more somber reflections on obstacles and attitudes of our unbecoming are not meant to discourage us, but rather to encourage us to refine our motives and goals as gold is refined in the crucible. Love is the great refiner. Jesus shows us by example how this works, as do many of the greats in history. Of course, there are the "nearly greats" who built big egos at the expense of those perceived as weak or powerless. When they came to crossroads of choice between growth and here-and-now glory, they caved in and lost the goal of true greatness, which is becoming one's own name, an integrated, caring human person who learns compassion by genuine reciprocal living.

Throughout the Spiritual Exercises, we meet self in an enlightened way through Jesus, who mirrors for us intimacy at its best. We look at what is primary – our priorities and proclivities – and come to an awareness of the pulls in this or that direction that make the journey hard and perilous but strangely sure. One trip with these Exercises is only the start of the process back to where we come from, Love, though this is not discernable at first glance. We usually want so much! And we usually want it all and don't realize when we have it within our reach.

Similar to the Ignatian Exercises, the exercises Progoff outlines in his book, *At a Journal Workshop,* are arranged to facilitate our engaging in our own growth and development so that a whole person, a holy person emerges. The Spiritual Exercises of St. Ignatius and those of Progoff's *Intensive Journal®* method lead us to enlightenment about the weaving of our life threads and how new decisions about living can energize and renew us.

We begin now to enter a deeper meditation on the patterns of our own living that have nurtured our becoming, and especially those crossroad decisions that may have sabotaged our sense of well-being.

Sabbath Time

At a Journal Workshop invites us to enter a "Sabbath time" – a time set apart – a sacred time. It is to be a time for reflection, data collecting, walking down memory lane, of opening doors to rooms that have been closed by seared memories or completely blocked memories, of gardens full of nosegays of joy and delight. All that and more happens during the Sabbath rest. The restful atmosphere is essential to the awakening awareness, for the true hearing/listening to the Self.

The Exercises of Ignatius and insights from Progoff help us to discern the workings of the development of our gifts and to channel the energy of destructive forces into a growth pattern that helps us move toward enlightenment and transformation. Our only task is to desire enlightenment and transformation with all our being. Desire is an open highway to deeper and deeper awareness of one's evolution as a person and a soul. The journey that is one's life is leading to awe, surprises, unknowns, encounter with fear, pain, joy, and opportunity for transformation.

A Journal Entry

As we write in this journal section, we date the pages with the day, date, and year. We begin with a direct experience of where we are now. The focus is now because now is where our experience is. The poet Rainer Maria Rilke once referred to God as "you Limitless Now" (Barrows and Macy 1996, p. 67). Now is a time for opening up present experiences in order to feel the movement of our life and what has gone into its present state of being. We begin in inner quiet in order to feel into our life now, asking the question, What is my life saying to me now? Let yourself feel into this time until you are ready to describe it in a few paragraphs.

When you have come to a stop, reread what is written, being aware of what feelings are present within. Jot these down, remembering a very important fact: the writing is for your eyes only. No one reads your journal notes. If you ever want someone to know what has happened to you, read it aloud to them and note as you do so any insights and awareness that come to you as a result of hearing what you wrote. Later, you will enlarge the picture of your life and its incidents.

The principle of journal work reflects the inner movement of each life on its own terms. It is your sense of the meaning of it all that is important. Another person who may have lived that time with you may express it in radically different terms. There is room for fluctuations in and multiple interpretations of our human existence. Jung once claimed that personal healing was not possible without the discovery of personal meaning in the depth of one's being.

Having grounded yourself more fully in the present by thoughtfully describing the now of your life, you are invited to articulate the deeper narrative of your life. You will be writing your life, so to speak. Each individual can experience a sense of the wholeness of her or his life in dynamic movement into the future, a future being born through all the events and influences leading to the present moment.

A *Kairos* Biography

We sit in quiet to access Sabbath rest. Enter inner stillness. Begin to distinguish inner time (qualitative and *kairos*) from outer time (quantitative and *chronos*). *Chronos* is the Greek word for clock time – the linear, one-dimensional passage of years. *Kairos* is qualitative or sacred time – moments in time that are life-changing or altering of one's consciousness.

Sitting in quiet inner silence, relaxed and nondirective, allow spontaneous phrases to emerge that describe moments and movements of your becoming who you are today, as well as events and seasons of your life that threatened your becoming, stymied your growth, or were experienced as the unraveling of your life. This should be done spontaneously and quickly since the information is so much a part of our lives. You may want to refer to track 7 on the CD.

After writing these *kairos* movements, moments, events or seasons reread them slowly, being aware of feelings, insights, or discoveries that may arise. Then briefly record the thoughts and feelings that stirred as you read to yourself what you have written. Note any insights, ideas, or feelings that arise as you re-read what you have written.

Again, there is no judgment to make. You are just noting your own reflective patterns. Always date your entry.

We are loosening the soil in our life to let in the sunlight of our intellect, the rain of wisdom, and the richness of our power of decision making, thus coming out of the darkness of punitive assessments. You are being invited to name and claim the threads of continuity in your own life.

The work needs to be gradual. You are involved in a loving look at the human landscape of your lived experience, full of hills, valleys, deserts, oceans, and mountains. All this is explored for its wealth of meaning, suffering, joys, and achievements. Our life is a remarkable journey as we travel it with openness. We can open closed doors, look at what is within to discover the secrets hidden, perhaps for years, and learn what they have to tell us through journal writing, inner dialogue, conversation with a spiritual mentor, or other means. Old wounds can be healed, love remembered, and previously avoided possibilities for growth embraced anew.

Entering Mystery

You are beginning to "notice" the mysterious twists and turns, the continuity of the threads that make your life your own weaving or tapestry. The Jesuit theologian Karl Rahner said, "Hence our deepest fundamental experience, what haunts the very roots of our being, is a God who remains *mystery*. This God communicates [God]self in such a way that [God's] specific will for the individual can be discovered" (quoted in Egan 1980, 99–112).

Our work is to discover the mystery of who we are.

> *The range of what we think and do is limited*
> *by what we fail to notice. And because we fail*
> *to notice that we fail to notice, there is little we*
> *can do to change until we notice how failing to notice*
> *shapes our thoughts and deeds.*
>
> —an R. D. Laing "Knot"

Notes

1. It may be of interest to the reader to know that, since 1998, Jesuit-sponsored Creighton University has offered the 19th Annotation of the Exercises in an online format called "An Online Retreat: A 34-week retreat for Everyday Life" with weekly guides, helps for prayer, and reflection provoking photographs at www.creighton.edu/ CollaborativeMinistry/online. *Ed.*

3. Incarnational Spirituality

❧

INCARNATIONAL SPIRITUALITY IS THE KIND OF SPIRITUALITY that blends Ignatian insight with holistic depth psychology. Before fleshing out the meaning of "incarnational" spirituality with a small *i*, it is important to first explore the importance of Incarnation from a specifically Christian point of view. The second week of the Ignatian Exercises is devoted to meditation and contemplation on the life of Jesus, and thus a theological grasp of the importance of the God-made-human in Jesus of Nazareth is essential for the Christian faith life.

That God became flesh in the historical Jesus of Nazareth is a central conviction of Christian faith. God became human. The Infinite took on the finite and dwelt with us, born as we are. In Jesus, God's free decision to enter human experience as human is revealed once in time for all time. God spoke an irrevocable Word in Jesus and took on the very flesh of humanity. Catholic theologian Richard McBrien says, "because of the Incarnation, God is in humankind and remains so for all eternity, and humankind is for all eternity the expression of the mystery of God because the whole human race has been assumed in the individual human reality of Jesus" (1994, p. 498).

God chose to self-disclose in the midst of the world where humans are most at home. God gave Godself to humanity in direct proximity. Therefore, for the Christian all ways of meeting God are personal. All the dimensions of our humanity, all our senses and our body, our emotions and intellect, all of creation and other human beings are vehicles of divine encounter. God's decision to continue the creative act of becoming by taking on the flesh and blood of human experience makes divinity tangible and underscores God's unceasing need to be close to God's creations.

Thus, Christians are called to live an incarnational spirituality, meaning we are involved in a lifelong process of giving birth to our potential for wholeness and holiness. Our destiny is the journey of giving birth and being born again and again. Incarnational spirituality is experienced, as Ignatius would say, by finding God in all things. As a Jew, Progoff most likely would not be inclined to use the term *incarnational* in the same sense as Ignatius or other Christian theologians. Yet his positive regard for all the experiences that go into a person's becoming, including the threats and defeats we face in our becoming, are for Progoff the very stuff that makes our lives so dynamically sacred.

Jesus as Bridge

Part of the mystery of human personhood is the ongoing reality of egos run amuck or grasping after personae that distort the true image of God each one of us is called to be and become. The Genesis story expresses this truth through the myth of Adam and Eve's misdirected choice to presume equality with God. Pandemonium resulted, causing the Trinity to look on their creation with alarm. The Trinity did not want the essentially good, beautiful, and sacred creation to be lost forever in a ruptured relationship with its Source of Life. So they chose to do some salvaging by way of the Incarnation. The Infinite took on the finite and dwelt with us, being born as we are, living as we do, and most of all, taking on the fullness of human nature.

The Great Council convened to consider the situation. You might say the Trinity had a board meeting to look over their investments. Where had they gone wrong? What to do to mend all the havoc? The Word – the Logos – was sent, clothed in the garment of human flesh, to show us the way to the fullness of life and living abundantly. Thus, Jesus of Nazareth became the bridge that provided humanity a route to reunion with God by way of healing, just, and right relationships with each other and all of creation. Jesus was the messenger of Good News. Incarnation (the act of taking on flesh) became a fact. The Word spoken as Abba's Son made him brother, friend, redeemer, the one who would walk with us to regain our capacity to live God's original intent for humanity.

The word that describes this faith-based reality is *incarnation*. Sad to say, a word bandied about, misconstrued, and glossed over. There is no way to exaggerate its importance in the actual practice of Christian faith. God chose to know, in the biblical sense of physical intimacy, what it means to be human. God's desire for an empathic relationship with us spilled out in birth. Incarnation is a celebration of God-with-us in the depths, heights, and dregs of our human experience, once in time and through all time. In Jesus, God experienced (as God did with Moses) the peaks of joy and valleys of suffering that are part and parcel of the human journey. In sum, humanness does not diminish the status of God, it helps describe it.

Incarnational spirituality is about a deep commitment to engage personally, that which holds us in bondage in order to embrace the route to our destiny, being-in-God, who is our Primary Ancestor. The garden path was set askew by choosing self (ego) over God (Self). Since we are God's handiwork, there was no way and is no way for us to regain our inheritance of God's reign of personal well-being and universal *shalom* without incarnational living. Even if it were possible for us never to make a misstep on the journey, we will never *be* God in perfect completeness in our temporal life. For Christians, the chasm between the Divine and human is "bridged" irrevocably by Jesus.

Here in time, we are celebrating the eternal birth which God the Father bore and bears unceasingly in eternity, because this same birth is now born in time, in human nature. St. Augustine says: "What does it avail me that this birth is always happening, if it does not happen in me? That it should happen in me is what matters."

—Meister Eckhart, from Sermons and Treatises, Vol. I, translated and edited by M. O. Walshe (1987), p. 1.

Entering into Contemplation

Whether or not you hold in faith the preceding beliefs about Jesus of Nazareth as God's Incarnation, you can benefit from contemplating the mystery of Jesus as a threshold into a spirituality that is incarnational.

While we have used the words *meditation* and *contemplation* somewhat interchangeably, at this point a nuance is in order. Ignatius of Loyola stressed that active imagination is essential to a lush interior life. Contemplation as distinct from meditation moves beyond mental engagements and affective awareness to actually employing, via the imagination, the use of all the senses as we enter Sabbath time. Ignatian incarnational spirituality invites the involvement of the whole person, moving us from our head into our whole being through contemplation via application of the senses. We have five outer senses of sight, smell, hearing, taste, and touch, as well as a matching set of inner senses.

Ignatius introduces the contemplation on the Incarnation found in Scripture by first asking what desires arise in us as we read select passages, and second, applying our five senses in the work of contemplation. Applying our inner senses in the act of contemplation means that we exercise our imagination in order to enter the biblical scene portrayed in the text. We allow our inner senses free reign in guiding us to visualize the characters in the scene, hear the tone of their words, and imbibe the whole atmosphere of the moment. We feel the intensities and desires of the characters in the biblical scene and make them our own.

An Exercise in Contemplation

A Journal Entry

In preparing to enter an experience of contemplation, we first return to the Ignatian understanding of the importance of the exercise of desire. Ignatius is insistent that as spiritual seekers we ask for what we want and desire as we enter a period of prayer, meditation, or contemplation. He knew how important it is to be *conscious of* desire, and also how necessary it is for us to *know what* we desire.

This desire is an inherent push in us to have what is essential to achieving integration, becoming our most authentic selves. Often we misinterpret what is meant by essential, especially if pain is involved. Some of us crave solace at all costs, desiring only to exist in a state of being free from all pain. This is not the kind of desire fitting to achieving spiritual growth. There is no shallow peace, no satiety in authentic desire. Desire is not about the experience of gratification, but about the willingness and openness to risk the process of becoming. Desire erupts from the longing to see, hear, smell, taste, and touch the *shalom* found when we know we are standing on holy ground.

Using the quieting and centering practices found on pages 19–21, or after listening to tracks 8 and 9 on the CD, enter a still point or Sabbath rest and quietly and carefully read the following passage from the Gospel of Mark (2:1–12 NJB):

> When he returned to Capernaum, some time later word went around that Jesus was in the house; and so many people collected that there was no room left, even in front of the door. He was preaching the word to them when some people came bringing him a paralytic carried by four people, but as they could not get the paralytic through the crowd, they stripped the roof over the place where Jesus was; and when they had made an opening, they lowered the stretcher on which the paralytic lay. Seeing their faith, Jesus said to the paralytic, "My child, your sins are forgiven." Now some of the scribes were sitting there, and they thought to themselves, "How can this man talk like that? He is being blasphemous. Who but God can forgive sins?" And at once, Jesus inwardly aware that this is what they were thinking, said to them, "Why do you have these thoughts in your hearts? Which of these is easier: to say to the paralytic, 'Your sins are forgiven' or to say, 'Get up, pick up your stretcher and walk'? But to prove to you that the Son of man has authority to forgive sins on earth" – he said to the paralytic – "I order you, get up, pick up your stretcher, and go off home." And the paralytic got up, and at once picked up the stretcher and walked out in front of everyone, so that they were all astonished and praised God saying, "We have never seen anything like this."

After this first reading of the text and relying on your attunement to both your outer and inner senses, attend to the thoughts, ideas, emotional feelings, or bodily sensations that surface. Without judgment or censoring, record your initial responses in your journal. Date your entry.

Return to the text and reread the passage. With whom do you find yourself identifying? Are you in the crowd? An onlooker? Are you *the* crowd? Do you identify with the small band of friends who have brought their paralyzed friend to Jesus in hopes of a healing? Which one of the four are you? Do you imagine yourself risking an attempt to make an opening in the roof to lower your friend down so Jesus might have compassion on her or his suffering? Are you Jesus? Are you the One moved by the compassion exhibited by the four or the pain of the paralytic? Do you feel a kinship with the scribe, sitting in the room, watching and judging what is being said and done? Do you sense an empathic connection with the paralytic, the powerlessness, and the paralyzing wound that has you lying flat on your back? Are you drawn to the moments of power: "Your sins are forgiven." "Get up, pick up your stretcher, and go home." Are you the voice that frees and heals? Are you the voice that judges and condemns? Are you the voice that hears the healing words of forgiveness and rediscovers the power to get up and go on with life?

Find your place in the scene and imaginatively enter the moment and be that person(s), in that place, living that life. Ignite within yourself the urge to be part of this biblical mystery. Become part of it. Using the gifts of your inner senses, see the place, the people, the atmosphere, the room, the roof being broken open. Hear the voices, the banter, the conversations. With your inner ears, hear Jesus speaking. See him catch a glimpse of the stretcher being lowered toward him over his head. Can you hear the tone of the angry scribes as they chastise him and call him a blasphemer? Smell the crowdedness of the room, the scent of the air, the earth and animal smells in Capernaum. Feel the press of the crowd, the urgency of the friends precariously holding the stretcher, the discomfort of the paralytic, the disorientation, fear, and hope when Jesus says, "rise, take your stretcher, and go home." Enter the astonishment.

When you are ready, write in free-flowing style in the first person all that is happening to you and in you as you enter this scene. Reread your entry. Make note of any surprises. Make note of any insight that seems significant to you. Date your entry.

The Way of Contemplation in
Incarnational Spirituality

The way to meet Jesus is first as a human person by entering deeply and intimately into his life experiences. Jesus' life is a mystery and so is ours. Contemplating the mysteries of Jesus' life is an aid to our learning more about our life. Each mystery becomes alive to us – incarnates – through the exercise of our capacity for imaginatively entering the scene, being there with the people, smelling the smells, experiencing the natural environment, seeing what is happening, hearing the words spoken, feeling the range of emotion. Our desire for an empathic passage into the sacred story holds the graced promise of a deep interior knowledge of Jesus and deepened intimacy with the relationship we seek in faith. All through the contemplation of the second week, Ignatius has us make this desire our greatest urge.

Having explored the contemplative method outlined above, you now can select any biblical passage on Jesus from page 39 and continue to experience contemplation on the life of Jesus as a way of meeting him again for the first time and, in doing so, meeting yourself.

An Ignatian Colloquy

The preceding experience is an important segue into Ignatius's use of *colloquy* as a distinctive prayer form. It is similar to Ira Progoff's development of the methods of inner dialogue in that both Ignatius and Progoff see great value in the capacity we have to engage in internal or interior conversational exchange.

First, we need to set the proper internal mood for the interior conversation. Find a place where you will not be interrupted, a place where you can quiet down from your haste and restlessness. Savor the silence of being quiet; savor your own inner peace. Put away all preoccupations, thoughts, musts, "have-to" and be attentive to the now. You may choose to return to the quieting and centering practices found on pages 19–21, leading you to a still point within, a Sabbath rest.

What are the relational situations that are claiming your time and energy? Is there an experience you are having in a relationship or with a group of people that springs to consciousness, such as planning a major celebration that requires consensus among very opinionated people, a workplace dilemma, an unhealed rupture in a friendship? It is important that you focus upon those relational situations that are of consequence in your life because the persons are important to you. Allow yourself to move into those situations that are inviting and loving as well as those that are annoying and discomforting. Make a list of what surfaces for you. Without censure or judgment, briefly describe these consequential relational situations, allowing your memory and imagination free reign. Record it as a journal entry. Date the entry.

After you have finished writing, reread your entry. Upon reflection, what relational situation seems to call out most for your attention? Pay special attention to that individual or situation you resist considering. Often, that which we resist is exactly what we need to consider. Select the person(s) to whom you will address yourself. Write a brief statement in your journal as to why you desire this meeting, such as, "I have chosen to engage [name] today because . . . ." Why it is important for you *today* to enter this conversation, or as Ignatius would say, have a colloquy with this particular person or these particular people?

You are now ready to experience a colloquy. Open your journal to a new page and determine how you will identify the other one or ones to whom you are speaking. Use an initial or "me" to denote yourself and another initial or symbol for the other. Allow the dialogue to come forth by itself, bubbling up without control, enforced direction, or censorship of any kind. Don't stop the flow of the exchange, even if something emerges that you don't want to hear or do not like. This is a free-flowing exchange. Allow the dialogue to continue to its natural conclusion. You may find that once you are into the exercise your writing cannot keep pace with the dialogue. Permit yourself to invite both your inner self and your dialogue partner to slow down so that all that needs to be said is given expression. There may be pauses in the banter. Do not force the conversation. Write when you are moved to do so. When the conversation appears to be ending, pay attention to how it draws to a close. Date the entry.

> *The Colloquy is made, properly speaking, as one friend*
> *speaks to another.*
>
> —Ignatius of Loyola (from Fleming 1996, p. 48)

Close your journal. Move out of the active contemplation to an inner closing meditation using music, a psalm, a body gesture that enables you to draw closure on this Sabbath time. If you feel drawn to reread the dialogue, do so and note in a new journal entry your reflections on the conversation.

Conclusion

At another time, you may wish to select a figure or group from the Gospel of Mark narrative used earlier in this chapter. You can initiate a colloquy with Jesus, the paralytic, the four friends, the crowd, or the scribes. You can deepen contemplation on you own life by working through each of the relational situations you identified and engaging each situation in the interior exercise of colloquy.

Week two of the Spiritual Exercises recommends contemplating the infancy narratives, as well as the following:

Mark 1, Luke 3 – Baptism of Jesus
Luke 1, 2, and 3 – The Hidden Life
Luke 4:1–13, Matthew 4:1–11 – Temptation of Jesus
John 1:35–51, Matthew 9:9, Mark 2:13–17, Luke 5:27–28 – Call
Matthew 5:5–7 – Sermon on the Mount.
Luke 5:1–11, Mark 1:16–20, Matthew 4:18–22 – The Unexpected Catch
Luke 8:22–25, Matthew 8:18, 23–27, Mark 4:35–41 – Storm on the Lake

It is possible, as well, to apply the above colloquy method to inanimate objects, such as the paralytic's stretcher, the wood beams, thatch on the roof, or other objects in the gospel narratives, such as a boat, the wind at sea, a net full of fish, or even the emotions of fear or astonishment. It is also possible to dialogue with an image that seems significant to you or an item of significance in your profession, such as a sewing machine, a canvas, a computer. One can dialogue with one's wheelchair or walker, the wedding ring of a deceased spouse, the saved letter from a first love. The imaginative possibilities are endless.

Ignatius and Progoff converge in their conviction that we can access deeper understanding about the thin threads that weave our life together and about God's loving design for us by exercising our imaginative capacities to "place" ourselves where we really need to be in order to grow. Such is the beauty, burden, and blessing of an incarnational spirituality.

4. The Shadow in Human Becoming

❖

IT HAS BEEN SAID THAT WHEN JESUS TURNED TO THE MULTITUDE and said, "Take up your cross and follow me," he was referring to our responsibility to carry the burden of our own personalities (Mk. 8:34; Mt. 16:24, Lk. 9:23). Since we possess the marvelous capacity to achieve the potentials planted by God deep within us, why is it that so many experience daily living as though they are carrying a weighty burden? Paul, in his letter to the Romans, says it this way: "I do not understand my own behavior; I do not act as I mean to, but I do things that I hate. While I am acting as I do not want to, I still acknowledge the Law as good, so it is not myself acting, but the sin which lives in me" (Rom. 7:15–17 NJB).

Might Paul be talking about Jung's notion of the shadow? In depth psychology, the shadow is the dumping ground for all the characteristics of our personality that we dislike, disown, and deny. These parts of ourselves, when left ignored and unaddressed, can sabotage our process of becoming. We shall see that the shadow can be extremely valuable to our experience of spiritual wholeness. Carrying the burden of our own shadow without "projecting" it out onto others is a spiritual discipline, a whole-making and sacred part of who we are. Since the shadow is actually more genuine than our persona, the face we show to the outer world, it also has been said that God loves the shadow more because it is more authentic (for a fuller explication of this notion, see Sanford 1993).

In Jungian theory, the persona, literally meaning, "mask," is the side of ourselves we allow others to see. It is our psychological clothing bearing the image we permit ourselves to reveal to the public. The ego carries our persona because the ego is what we know consciously. The shadow, on the other hand, is that part of our personality that we fail to see or know because we relegate its unacceptable features to unconsciousness. Shadow refers to that part of the personality that we have repressed for the sake of the ego ideal. But the refused and unwanted dimensions of who we are do not evaporate; they only collect in the dark corners of our psyche, often waiting to play themselves out destructively.

This is what is meant by projection: the tendency to see our shadow "out there" in others who become the repository of the disdain we are unwilling to examine within ourselves. We think that we have "buried alive" these parts of who and how we are, but they often emerge when we least expect it. Psychologically, the shadow will claim its due, and when allowed to accumulate and go unattended, it will spill out in self-defeating and alienating ways. Owning our own shadow is a requisite for finding true wholeness and healing.

We cannot escape the dark side of who we are, but as Jungian psychologist Robert Johnson says, we can pay it out intelligently (1991, p. 15), meaning, we take responsibility for it and do conscious work on it instead of laying it on someone or something else. Projection manifests itself in the form of excessive anger, vengeful thinking and acting, scapegoating, blaming, cruelty, prejudice, verbal/emotional abuse, and intolerance. Dishonoring our shadow by refusing to deal with its presence within our personality also results in depression, ennui, inner emptiness, and inability to establish mutuality in relationships, self-absorption, and psychosomatic illnesses. Jung used to say that we could be grateful to those whom we make our enemies, for their darkness allows us to escape our own (Johnson 1991, p. 37).

The paradox is that living an incarnational spirituality is not possible if one is unwilling to bring to birth the beast along with the beauty. Jungian analyst and scholar Murray Stein aptly calls the shadow "the image of ourselves that slides along behind us as we walk toward the light" (1998a, p. 88). "In the showdown, God (Self) favors the shadow over the ego, for the shadow with all its dangerousness is closer to the center and more genuine" (Johnson 1991, pp. 44–45). Anything brought forth from the shadow into the light holds the potential to become light itself.

> *... but anything shown up by the light will be illuminated and anything illuminated is itself light.*
>
> —Ephesians 5:13 NJB

> *Knowing your own darkness is the best method for dealing with the darknesses of other people.*
>
> —C.G. Jung (from *Letters,* vol. 1, pp. 236–7)

Befriending Your Shadow
A Journal Exercise

Please allow a full hour to engage in the following exercise. This exercise will be of maximum benefit if you create for yourself a Sabbath time without interruptions in order to complete all of the steps in the meditation in the same sitting.

Open your journal and record at the top of a clean page, "Me and My Shadow." Date your entry.

Take sufficient time to cross the threshold into a sacred stillness.

Express your desire to meet your shadow unafraid, to connect with and claim your rejected qualities, to carry the burden of your own personality, to mine the gold from the shadow that is so genuine and important to your full becoming. Ask for the desire to honor your shadow.

Enter into the inner honesty where you admit to yourself that you have some conscious awareness of your darker side. Remember, the shadow itself is neither sinister nor sinful; it is your refusal to own your own shadow that causes so much mischief in your life.

Choose to come full face with your shadow in order to take it back into your psychic structure – where it first originated and where it is required for your wholeness. Invite it into your consciousness so that you don't have to fear projecting it out onto others in self-defeating and relationally unhealthy ways.

As you continue to enter more deeply into a focused twilight state, become very quiet and allow your own shadow to emerge into greater consciousness and clarity.

When you feel ready, and without self-recrimination, judgment, censoring, justifying, or any filtering, record in your journal how you experience the shadow dimension of your personality.

Is there an image, metaphor or single word that best captures your experience of your own shadow?

Make a list of your shadow characteristics.

Maintaining the atmosphere of sacred time and space, enter into your emotional or affective response to facing into your shadow. How do you feel about yourself as you own your own shadow? Feel your feelings. Without censure or self-critique, simply record the feelings and insights that surface at this time.

You may want to stand, aware of your own feelings and body sensations, honor your shadow by making a deep bow, a gesture of reverence, before this *sacra pagina* (sacred page).

Notice what is happening with all your inner senses. Record any observations.

Seated again, review the manifestations you have listed that disclose the characteristics of your shadow. What particular shadow characteristic stands out for you now as the one you are drawn toward in this moment in time?

Select a single shadow characteristic and record why it is that this dimension of your personality "speaks" to you at this time? Why is it that you are being drawn toward this dimension of your shadow?

Now, to the best of your ability, record the development in the life of this characteristic in your personality, what influenced its development, how it most poignantly manifests itself in your life, what benefit it is to you, and the difficulty it provokes.

Feel the movement in the life story of this part of your shadow and identify those steps in its life that strike you as most significant today. Let yourself be free to perceive them as they emerge without critique or defense.

When you have finished, put down your pen, close your eyes and feel the presence of the whole life of your shadow and claim it as your own. You may choose to involve your body by standing and cradling your shadow close to yourself in a gesture of embrace. Now walk around the room, as if you were holding and soothing a baby.

When you have completed this physical embrace of your shadow, record any observations about the experience of this ritual of embrace.

Now, enter into a colloquy with your shadow characteristic. Follow the directions for preparing for a colloquy as described on page 37–38. Remember this is free-flowing conversation. Identify yourself as "me" and name the shadow characteristic as your dialogue partner. Greet your shadow and invite the conversation. You speak and let the shadow speak. Allow the conversation to have a life of its own. Record all that is said until all that desires to be expressed has been said.

When the conversation has finished put your pen down and inwardly remember what was said. Drink it in.

Record any observations you may have about what you have just read. Do not edit the original colloquy in any way. Note any further reflections that surface in the form of additional thoughts, ideas, feeling, surprises, or disturbances. Date your entry.

Conclude the meditation session by closing your journal and acknowledging the fact that in some measure you have laid claim to your own shadow. Quietly consider that God favors the shadow over the ego because it is closer to the center and more genuine.

In silence, listen to the following:

Whatever is brought into the light becomes light itself.

Say aloud (as many times as you choose):

Whatever is brought into the light becomes light itself.

The last time you choose to say this verse aloud, end with "Amen." This concludes the meditation.

At another time you can return, review your inner work, and select another aspect of your shadow to engage by moving through the same process. The danger we fear in looking at these alien aspects of ourselves is that they will overwhelm us and put us into a funk from which we will not be able to recover; on the other hand, the consequences of refusing to take ownership of our shadow can ultimately be far greater.

The seed of life in the darkness is stronger than the entire darkness.

—Marie-Louise von Franz

5. Meeting the Forces of Good and Evil

I N THE SECOND WEEK OF THE SPIRITUAL EXERCISES, IGNATIUS presents the confrontation with the Two Standards – the dynamic of good and evil in human conscience (see nos. 136–148 in Fleming 1996). Without the benefit of the insights of modern depth psychology, Ignatius was a deft spiritual traveler into the profound inner experience of the life-giving and death-dealing forces at play in our process of becoming. Progoff suggests that serious inner work cannot take place unless we accept and confront the shadow side of our personality. As already noted, the shadow in human personality is itself not sinful or evil. It is the consequences of not dealing with it, as we have already suggested, that result in un-becoming, potentially destructive, patterns of living.

Put in modern language, we are seriously considering the truth of the pull of opposites that Paul so vividly described in Romans 7:15–17. He laments the fact that what he wants to do, he fails to do, and what he does not want to do, he succumbs to, as do all of us. The fact that this is a true statement regarding human nature lends credence to Jung's notion of the collective shadow. For Jung, the reality of the shadow in human personality had frightening consequences because so many individuals refused to recognize its existence. In doing so, the "little weaknesses and foibles" of human personality carried the dramatic, even demonic, potentiality to erupt in a collective or cultural expression of inhumanity.[1] If we do not wake up and separate ourselves from the collective shadow, we contribute to its destructive life force in the world.

The sixteenth-century vocabulary, imagery, and idiom of Ignatius are strange to our modern ways of speaking about this real and frightening reality. Ignatius speaks of Christ as Leader and Lord, the Commander-in-Chief, who does combat with Lucifer, the demonic enemy of humankind. Ignatius's imagery arises from his own experience as a warrior doing battle against an enemy. The devil, the opposite of the Creator of all Life, is the one who sums up all the evils that beset humanity. The devil becomes the collective sum of all the dark and unredeemed parts we refuse to bring to light.

Lucifer is the personification of the mortal enemy of human nature. Falling prey to the forces of Darkness allows the Demon to insidiously undermine our equilibrium, wreak havoc, create inner chaos, and birth only despair. Everything about Lucifer is false, including the name itself, which means "bearer of light." The Evil One is the hostile opposite of God's incarnation in Jesus, the Christ (meaning "the anointed one"), the true light come into the world.

Ignatius presents Jesus, the true standard, as an outstanding model for real living. The Prince of Peace is a counterpoint to the Prince of Darkness. Lucifer or Satan is the opposing false standard, the negative exemplar of all that is the opposite of good. Satan lures and seduces us away from the way, truth, and life through subtle and devious methods. Ignatius mentions the human tendency to covet what does not belong to one, to lust after positions of power and prestige at the expense of others and the common good.[2] The third and most destructive lure is succumbing to pride, the abdication of the virtues of humility and compassion and the fall into a life of excessive self-absorption and personal aggrandizement.

We all want the successful, convenient, and comfortable life that is presented to us every minute of every day as necessary to our well-being by the print and electronic media. In the United States, we have been driven by a sense of the American dream as our birthright; often numbing us to anguished cries of sisters and brothers in other locations whose privation is directly related to our satiation. We are inundated with superficial lures whose chime is summed up in the words, "I want, I deserve, I am entitled to . . . ."

Jesus, the principle of abundant life, pulls us in the opposite direction. He is "the way, the truth and the life" (Jn. 14:6). He is "the

Light of the world . . . who follows me will not walk in darkness, but will have the light of life" (Jn. 8:12, 12:35–36, 46). How do we follow this standard? How do we know if we are in the way and ways of Jesus? Contemplation on Matthew 25, Luke 7:18–50, and the First Letter of John provide the answer. We shall return to these texts in the applied section of this chapter. Suffice to acknowledge here that the way and ways of Jesus have to do with embracing the great commandment: loving God with your whole heart, mind, and soul and your neighbor as yourself (Dt. 6:4–9 and Mt. 22:37–39).

In holistic depth-psychological terms, this means doing the hard and hopeful work of finding *love all around us in disguise*. It is about unmasking what is false, superficial, and deceitful. It means practicing the truth that the Center of all Life and Love resides within, yet is not oneself but the Self, God. The tendency to hubris is replaced by desire for humility. You will meet this Center of Life and Love most dramatically enfleshed in others, the gift of relationships where you can come to be who you truly are meant to be in intimacy and mutuality. Interpersonal relationships are the richest environments for growth. Because of grace, freedom, and the standard of Jesus, you can take responsibility for bearing the cross of your own personality as a path to life and life abundant (Jn. 10:10). And through your desire to follow him, you can develop the strength of compassion to feel with others in their pain and promise.

You are a caretaker, not an owner, and as a caretaker you will not prevent the poor from exercising their right to enjoy life's fullness and to have shelter from the elements, healing from sickness, and protections from danger. You will not covet but be a seeker for justice, meaning you will find out what belongs to whom and give it back. As a steward, you will strive for dominion with and reverence for all of creation given into your care.

Thus, the two standards are two ways of life put before us. The pull of opposites is a mighty force. We can no more stop the movement of opposing forces than we can prevent the pull of gravity by human exertion or will. Without God's divine energy (grace) we would never become the sharing, loving, fully developed persons we are called and gifted to become.

An Extended Meditation on the Implications of Spiritual Engagement with the Two Standards in Making Life-giving Decisions

Review pages 19–21 or listen to the CD and prepare to enter a period of inner stillness. Follow the quieting exercises that create the outer and inner condition of receptivity needed for contemplation.

As previously mentioned, Ignatius uses the term *colloquy* as a distinctive prayer form. Developing the interior skill of colloquy enhances the richness of your inner world and its workings. You are invited to explore three brief colloquies as part of gathering the desire to enter more deeply into relationship with Depth.

When one enters either the preparatory period in anticipation of meditating or contemplating or is engaged in the actual experience of the meditation or contemplation time, as we usually understand it ceases to have meaning. Therefore, it is not important to put a time limit on "three brief colloquies." Suffice it to say that what follows are preparatory meditations leading to a deeper prayerful consideration of life choices and life direction.

1. Imagine Mary, woman of Nazareth and mother of God. Pause for a few moments to capture a visual image or use a visual image of Mary significant to you. This may be an image of a young or middle-aged Mary, an icon of Mary, the Mother of Perpetual Help, Mother of the Disappeared, Our Lady of Guadalupe, Michelangelo's "Pieta," or a Black Madonna. You may choose to begin your colloquy with listening to a recording of "Ave Maria" or a Marian hymn that has meaning for you. You may decide to sing the hymn or song as part of your quieting into meditation.

   When you sense you are in company with Mary, ask for the desire to embrace the insight and challenges of life choices that currently tug at your attention. Ask her to release within you her gifts of inner receptivity and courage to bear forth light against any prevailing darkness.

   As you ask Mary, listen to her responses arising in you, which may, of course, be heard as pregnant silence. Record the fruits of your colloquy. Date your entry.

2. Follow the same pattern and now invite Jesus, born of Mary, son of Joseph, Word made flesh, to join you for a colloquy. Allow your imagination to give a face to Jesus or select an image that is meaningful for you. You may choose to light a candle to ritualize the presence in your midst of the Light of the World illuminating any obstacles that might prevent seeing Jesus in order to have a face-to-face conversation with him. Slowly read the brief five chapters of the First Letter of John in expectation of the kind of self-honesty you desire to bring to conversation with the Word.

When you sense his company, repeat your request for desire to resist the lures of material satiation, greed, power, and prestige (Luke 4:1–13). Ask to know the truth so that the truth will set you free (John 8:31).

You have used enough words now. Rest in the Word and listen Jesus into speech. Record the fruits of your colloquy. Date your entry.

3. Enter into the third and final colloquy with *Abba*. *Abba* is the Aramaic word recorded in the gospels as one of the words Jesus used to speak of and to Yahweh. This word expresses the very intimate relationship Jesus experienced with God and was the word used to address God in early Christian communities (see Galatians 4:6 and Romans 8:15).

Enter the space of radical humility and absolute child-like simplicity as if you were pulling on the hem of your mother's skirt or tugging at your Daddy's pant leg to get her or his attention. Ask *Abba* for what it is you need this very moment to help you be still enough to hear what it is you need to hear. And if your confusion or fear is great, permit yourself the release of tears or the welling up and spilling over a big wail and let *Abba* do the rest. Record the fruits of your colloquy. Date your entry.

Review the respective fruits of the triple colloquy and without self-censure or judgment note any surprises or particularly important observations. As with Ignatius, your journal is to be your constant companion, the
sacra pagina, the recorded truth of your experience. Date your entry.

A Foray into Humility

To assist the pilgrim in faith in making a decision about a life path
or *election,* the term Ignatius uses, it is profitable to pause and mull
over the three kinds of humility suggested by Ignatius. Humility is
an oft abused and even more misunderstood virtue. It derives from
the Latin *humus,* meaning "the substance of mother earth, the soil,
without which the forest could not survive." The earth itself is a vast
container of moisture and nutrients keeping the floor of the forest
alive. The floor of the forest is its place.

In St. Catherine of Siena's (1347–1380) *Dialogues* (Thorald 1943), she
addresses the virtue of humility. Humility helps us know our place as
creatures before the Creator. If we truly desire to know ourselves, we
simultaneously enter into the mystery of God's own nature, in whose
image we are created. This truth keeps us in the place from which we
can best give and receive the nurture always spiritually surrounding us.
Even arid desert regions abounding in sand possess a vibrant ecosys-
tem that is sustaining.

Humility flows naturally from the human spirit. Pride arises from
a distortion of our true natures. Pride, as the opposite of humility,
creeps around in shadow and, when left unattended, saps authenticity and drains us of our truth. To be humble is to live as close to the
truth as possible: to be one with all creation in praising and rever-
encing life as the gift of God that it is each day, today and forever.

Ignatius provides some descriptions on the spectrum of humility.
The first kind of humility is about living in such a way as not to turn
one's back on God or make a radical choice in the direction of un-
becoming. The second kind of humility is reflected in the desire to
live to do the will of Abba. The unfolding of God's will is revealed as
God's loving design for the fullness of our becoming. Living in this
sense of trust enables a person to experience an equilibrium that
mitigates against the extremes of grasping after everything or, on the

other hand, abdicating personal responsibility for accomplishing anything. The third kind of humility faces the seeker for this virtue with the most radical response – to live as close to the truth of Jesus' life as humanly possible. To be so moved as to follow Jesus in radical dispossession and live in solidarity with God's poor (Fleming 1996, pp. 128–131). Meditating on the continuum of humility leads one in the direction of making choices of ultimate concern.

Times of transition or crisis bring us face to face with many alternatives. There is more than one signpost with our name suggesting the sometimes too many forks in life's road. Deep in our nature is the desire to become a fully integrated person. Such integration is achieved in humility as one risks the fragile exercise of one's freedom to determine which way to go. A human person is an extraordinary being with great power, yet so vulnerable that one can be struck down and disoriented in an instant by a single smooth stone, properly aimed (I Sam. 17:40, 48–49). Thus, facing into the forces that arise to thwart our growth and mustering the courage to cast our life's lot in the direction of Love is the inescapable reality of living the life that wants to live in us.

The Fundamental Option

Sixteenth-century Ignatius would be right at home in affirming the modern theological anthropology of his spiritual son, Jesuit theologian Karl Rahner (1904–1984). Rahner's theological vision of the human person parallels Ignatius's conviction, which is truly a catholic conviction, that each person possesses an ultimate aim planted deep within human being. That aim is God, the Ultimate Horizon, Incomprehensible Mystery, Ground of Being. There is within each person, so to speak, a built-in transcendental orientation. There exists within the person a preapprehension, pregrasp, or predisposition (St. Bonaventure referred to it as contuition), which functions to move us naturally in the direction of the Horizon. This innate dynamic places the human (finite) in the direction of the infinite (God). Finite beings strive toward, move, grow, yearn, struggle, and reach out for the more of the Infinite.

It is not a given, however, that this natural striving results in our becoming spiritual beings. We possess the condition for that possibility. In the end, it is the exercise of our human freedom and our openness and responsiveness to the gift of grace that results in the actual unfolding of an ongoing relationship with the subject of our yearning. We choose in freedom and grace to make a *fundamental option* (see Rahner 1969b, pp. 181–188), disposing ourselves freely and forever in the direction of the Horizon. This decision is so fundamental to our self-understanding and so decisive as to forever determine our choice for God. It is the choice at the root of all subsequent choices. Thus, it is the ultimate election beneath all subsequent life elections. When we make this most primary election for God, though seasons of disorientation prevail, mistakes are made, and sin enters the patterns of our living, fundamentally there is never a question that it is God to whom we ultimately belong and will be reunited when we pass in death from this side to the other side.

Most, if not all persons, who would choose to engage such a book as this have made the act of humility, of the fundamental option of which we speak.

An Exercise in Remembering and Re-experiencing the Fundamental Option

Pause for a moment of quiet to recollect the tenor and tone of the triple colloquy. Their presence has not left your inner atmosphere. All you need do is close your eyes and allow your awareness of their presence as the quietness deepens. Let your breathing slow down. Be aware of letting your breathing slow down. Breathe in and out slowly. Gently go down into your own silence, your own solitude, down, down, deep into yourself – to the center of your being, the place of your life force. Be aware of letting your breathing slow down and of entering your silence. Be aware of thoughts going on in your head. Be aware of them and let them go. Be aware of the imaged being conjured up by your imagination. Be aware of the images and let them go. Be aware of the noises inside or outside the room or place you are in. Be aware and let these go. If people are around you, be intensively aware of their presence. Be intensively aware and let them go. Enter deeply into yourself, into your own solitude. Listen and hear.

In an atmosphere of deep silence, recall all the memories that appear when you imagine of time of making a fundamental option. As they surface, note them in your journal in free-flowing style. There is no need to attend to chronological order. Let them flow unsystematically.

Leave enough room to return to each to add more detail at a later date. At this time, just allow them all to rush forward and announce themselves to you without any need to organize or control them in any way. Know that they may be pleasant or painful.

As these recollections come to consciousness, describe them briefly, with just enough words to identify the memory sufficiently. You are collecting as many memories as you can. As they begin to stop "popping," go with the rhythm of slowing down until there seems to be no more kernels to notice. Put your pen down and rest in the overview of what you have collected.

Allow the memories to naturally place themselves in a sense of their importance to you today. Is there a standout memory? One recollection that most poignantly speaks to you today about the experience of making a fundamental option? Is there a memory at deeper glance that speaks to you about your spiritual awakening that is at the depth of your choice for God as fundamental to you as breathing in and breathing out?

Select that one memory and copy it again on a new journal page. Carefully examine what you have written about the memory you have selected. In free-flowing uncensored writing explore this story of your fundamental option in as much detail as possible without regard for any special organization of thought. When you have finished this focused writing, stop and reread what you have written. You are looking to note key happenings or events that preceded, defined, and shaped this single, powerful memory.

You are paying attention to the inner movements of a depth relationship with Depth.

Both Ignatius and Progoff knew it is essentially important to pay attention to inner movements, to that which is not conscious until you raise it gently up from the deep seas of your unconscious, like a great vessel buried with hidden treasures.

Record anything that stirred within you as you reread – feelings, insights, or surprises that emerge as you drink in this magnification of your spiritual history.

You may notice that you left out something that in reflection seems important to you now. Simply note what you noticed. Or you may be aware of an inclusion that now surprises you in some way. Without judgment or self-censure, simply note what you notice. Date your entry.

Now permit yourself to feel the authentic joy that comes with knowing that no matter what and through it all your fundamental choice to live your life in the direction of the Ultimate Horizon remains a constituent part of your daily living.

Conclude this period of meditation with a thought adapted from the writings of Karl Rahner, son of Ignatius, follower of Jesus, and appreciator of the human and personality sciences:

> We will forever wonder whether men and women have naturally received their finality toward the infinite for no other purpose than to roam forever, perpetual wanderers, through the domain of the finite, in order to greet the Infinite always only from afar, without ever discovering that direct road that would lead them to the face of God. (Quoted in McCool 1975, p. 30)

Rest in the knowing that while we all may be perpetual wanderers, roaming forever down the narrow and wide roads of our living, the Infinite/Intimate One is with us no matter what and through it all. The living out of our fundamental option is the mysterious winding road that leads us to the face of God.

Notes

1. For example, annihilation of the twin towers of the World Trade Center and thousands of people on September 11, 2001, in New York City, the Holocaust or Shoah, historical institutionalized slavery, genocide, modern racism and hate crimes. *Ed.*

2. For a discussion on the meaning of spiritual detachment see Jane Madejczyk, OSF, in "Loving Life: A Result of Facing Reality" (Clendenen 2002, pp. 47–52).

6. Suffering and Creativity

Introduction

IN THE OPENING WORDS OF HIS SUCCESSFUL BOOK, *The Road Less Traveled,* Scott Peck said simply, "Life is difficult" (1978, p. 15). Meditation and contemplation on suffering and its place in our life is rarely a consideration we relish. Yet resistance to facing our own experience of suffering keeps us from entering the "narrow way" toward wholeness and holiness. The third week of the Spiritual Exercises invites us into contemplation on the passion of Jesus. The word *passion* derives from the Latin *passio* and the Greek *pathos,* both meaning suffering. The passion of Jesus, which includes the Last Supper and the agony in the garden, becomes a metaphor for a final cleansing that clears the way for Jesus' embrace of the defeat on the cross, which is, in the experience of faith, the triumph of life in disguise. Jung once said that even a happy life couldn't be lived without a measure of sadness. The word *happiness* would lose its meaning if it were not balanced by sadness (see "A Spirituality of Balance" by Michael Cooper, SJ, in Clendenen 2002, pp. 53–67). In a culture that encourages us to anesthetize ourselves from pain, the Christian story illumined by the insights of depth psychology clearly suggests that working with our suffering – embracing the mystery and meaning of our *pathos* – is an essential companion to spiritual growth.

> *Life demands for its completion and fulfilment a balance between joy and sorrow.*
>
> —C. G. Jung
> (from "Psychotherapy and a Philosophy of Life," par. 185)

In common parlance, we say that each person has a threshold of pain. The term *threshold* is understood as both a point of entrance and the point at which a stimulus is, physiologically and psychologically speaking, of sufficient intensity to begin to produce an effect. From a spiritual point of view, the gravest difficulties that beset a person also open a door; create a threshold of vulnerability, which when entered holds promises beyond our comprehension. Emotional and spiritual breakthroughs often appear under the guise of suffering. Life is indeed difficult. The sadness of Jesus' final meal and the agonizing loneliness and desolation in the garden of Gethsemane is the mysteriously necessary prelude to the transforming force of the Resurrection. The considerations of this chapter parallel the challenging third week of the Ignatian exercises, providing the spiritual sojourner with new invitations for spirituality in depth.

There are many reasons why it is significant that Jesus' profound inner suffering takes place in a garden. The natural world of the garden suggests the fecundity and creativity waiting to emerge as each season uniquely unfolds, announces its distinct beauty, and passes into the next. The barrenness of winter holds the deeply embedded greenness waiting to spring forth; the cycle of birth and death played out on nature's stage is emblematic of our own lives. There is no way around it. The threshold is there for the crossing. Suffering, life's *pathos,* is a human gate to wider and richer human and spiritual experience.

History is replete with illustrations of the paradox of new life emerging from seeming death. Ancient mythology and the Hebrew and Christian scriptures provide apt examples. The mythological image of the phoenix has been a truth-telling story for millennia. The phoenix is a bird of great beauty, fabled to live more than five hundred years, burn itself to death, and then rise from its ashes in the freshness of new birth and begin another life cycle. Another example can be found in the Hebrew Bible when the prophet Ezekiel announces the explosion of breath and flesh from which a living army takes form amidst the valley of dry bones (Ezek. 37:1–14 NRSV):

The hand of the Lord was upon me, and brought me out by the Spirit, and set me down in the midst of the valley; it was full of bones. I was led around them; and behold, there were many upon the valley; and lo, they were very dry. And the Lord said to me, "Son of man, can these bones live?" And I answered, "O Lord God, only you know." The Lord said to me, "Prophesy to these bones, and say to them: O dry bones, hear the word of the Lord. Thus says the Lord God to these bones: Behold I will cause breath to enter you, and you shall live. And I will lay sinews upon you, and will cause flesh to come upon you, and cover you with skin, and put breath in you, and you shall live; and you shall know that I am the Lord."

In the Second Letter of Paul to the people of Corinth, we hear Paul's words of encouragement to those who are suffering. He admonishes them to embrace the paradox at the heart of Christian spirituality:

... through great endurance, in afflictions, hardships, calamities, beatings, imprisonments, tumults, labors, watching, hunger; by purity, knowledge, forbearance, kindness, the Holy Spirit, genuine love, truthful speech, and the power of God ... We are treated as imposters, and yet are true; as unknown, and yet well known; as said to be dying, but behold we live on; as punished, yet not killed; thought to be miserable, yet we are always rejoicing; taken for paupers though we make others rich; as having nothing, and yet possessing everything. (2 Cor. 6:4–10 NRSV)

Our human suffering is both real and a guise of something more. In Christian life, we call this the paschal mystery. The passion of Jesus – his final meal, agony in the garden, humiliation and crucifixion, and rising to new life – is how we understand the spirituality of the paschal mystery whereby God's eternally vivifying nature unmasks even the finality of death. *Pathos* becomes *mythos* and the shaping story of it all pulls us across the threshold of pain into a new level of consciousness.

> There is no birth of consciousness without pain.
>
> —C. G. Jung
>> (from "Marriage as a Psychological Relationship," par. 331)

Betrayal as Central Motif

It is of great significance, as noted earlier, that the story of the passion of Jesus includes an agonizing pause in a garden. It is in the garden that Judas betrays Jesus. The garden of Gethsemane is reminiscent of the Garden of Eden, where, mythically speaking, the primal betrayal takes place, which inaugurates the rupture that Christian faith has come to name the origin of sin. The primal trust between the Creator God and God's 'adam, God's earth-creatures, is broken. Original sin can be understood as a profound estrangement from our essence from which we never completely collectively heal. We live within the condition of the reality of sin and must consciously work against its negative effects.

The great myth of original sin teaches us that human beings, as images of God's own divine nature, are created in absolute freedom and can exercise their freedom in making choices that bring about healing and wholeness or produce alienation and estrangement. We have the capacities to deepen the bonds of love and trust or to betray that which we hold most dear. While God's covenantal love for creation and all living creatures always remains intact, relationship with God is a matter of human choice. Due to the power and possibility of the gift of freedom, there can be no coercion in relationship with God. Coercion is antithetical to interpersonal love. Human beings live as much in the condition of freedom and grace as we do in the lure to self-absorption, abuse of power, moral righteousness, intolerance, and deceit. Life is difficult and while some measure of deep sadness is inevitable, the reality of grace is the spiritual dynamism that pulls our struggling finite selves in the direction of the healing horizon of the Infinite. Paul prays this prayer for the people of Ephesus:

Out of God's infinite glory, may you be given the power through
God's Spirit for your hidden selves to grow strong, so that Christ
may live in your hearts through faith; and that you, being rooted
and grounded in love, may have the power to comprehend with all
the saints what is the breadth and length and height and depth, and
to know the love of Christ, which surpasses knowledge, that you
may be filled with all the fullness of God. (Eph. 3:16–19 NRSV)

These convictions form a framework for considering the sacred
wounds of betrayal, sometimes self-inflicted, which are so much
part of the universal fabric of human existence.

Exploring Connections Between Suffering and Creativity

A desire to listen to God and develop a relationship with our interior life tempers the strident voice of the ego. The more focused and
centered we become, the more Light will illumine the darker
dimensions of our life journey. I refer to this conscious engagement
with our inner self as a cleaning up of our inner atmosphere
through increased self-knowledge with the consequent growth in
love of self, which is healthy, affirming, and nourishing for the
sojourn into the desert of our lived experience. All birth and
growth is accompanied by a measure of pain, which holds the
promise of strengthening our inner self and releasing new creative
forces. Creative suffering is essential to the process of becoming a
self "filled with all the fullness of God."

Most people have experienced some form of betrayal: a disillu-
sionment of hopes or expectations in oneself, another, or God; a
radical rupture of trust in a relationship of significance, including
one's relationship with the Divine; an undeserved infidelity; a personal act of disloyalty; a grievous deception with destructive consequences; an unexposed lie buried deep in one's memory; the realization of a life unlived, talents not expressed, or potentials
untapped. The list of how we have encountered or experienced
betrayal is both common to many and uniquely known to us. Our
most critical wounding occurs around the issue of betrayal precise-

ly because it marks the severing of a trust held sacred. In some ways, exploring our personal experience of betrayal enables us to relate to the mythical experience of the biblical Fall when a radical rupture of covenantal relationship in the garden of harmony leads to the introduction of the condition of alienation and estrangement from which humanity has never escaped. When we meet the experience of brokenness we come face to face with our own capacities for being a proverbial Judas or a sleeping disciple unable to stay awake in the midst of a friend's dark night of the soul.

Hopefully, the exercises thus far in this book have enabled you to see and experience more conscious connections in the external and internal events – moments and movements – that are part of your evolution to the *now* of your life. There are thin threads of continuity weaving through past experiences into the now and future of one's life. It is a tenet of the science of the human psyche that memories which carry painful content need to be recalled and brought to consciousness in order to be integrated into the deeper continuity of one's life. Progoff says that as we recall and record such experiences we realize that the continuity of the whole of our outer and inner lives would not have been possible without *all* the events that have shaped us, including those barely noticed at the time they took place. Most importantly, he says that we must consider the implications of the fact that some of the ultimately most growth-filled of our life events were ones we would have avoided if we could have (Progoff 1992, p. 290). Has there not been a time when we, like Jesus in the garden, pleaded that the cup be taken from us? Those seeking fuller spiritual consciousness are invited to recognize the most unwanted, sometimes undeserved, events that belong to our spiritual journey.

A Mantra Meditation Exercise

A mantra, most often associated with Hinduism or Buddhism, is a sacred word or formula repeated, almost as an incantation. Mantras, however, can be a single word, a sound, a chime, a chant, or an object. Used here, a mantra refers to anything that serves as an aid to the quieting of the self. It is a means to the climate of inner stillness that creates the condition for the inner senses to be awakened. You will be invited in this meditation to create a mantra from the contents of your own life, by way of the areas in your life that were times of suffering. Out of suffering we learn more about life, life in the raw, and about the healing that is hidden in the suffering, if we can muster the courage to endure it and walk its narrow way.

Progoff says that suffering in our lives are the desert areas. As we come in touch with the desert areas we move through looking for oasis, places to find sufficient nourishment to sustain us. We come at last to the foothills of the mountain, and we begin to climb until we reach the face of God. Then we go down the other side of the mountain, into yet another desert and up yet another mountain. We always meet God. This is the divine biorhythm available to us if we are entering into our lives in a proper fashion, proper fashion meaning with openness. There are three words that provide keys to living our spiritual lives in the proper fashion of a spiritual seeker: (1) expectancy, (2) openness, and (3) vulnerability. Expectancy means to live in such a way as to allow for the unexpected in life. And when the unexpected happens, we can move with it, like a willow tree that bends with the wind and does not snap. In openness we can receive what life brings us and embrace it, while vulnerability is the condition in which this kind of living can happen. Being vulnerable nurtures the capacity for living the height and depth, breadth and scope of our own humanity. It is from the core of our vulnerability that we can experience healing within ourselves, which in turn overflows from us as a source of healing for others.

Before beginning a meditation period reflect on the following questions (you may listen to track 11 on the CD): How well am I living with expectancy? Do I move with grace in responding to the unexpected? Am I resistant to being a willow in the wind? Or, as twelfth-century Benedictine abbess Hildegard of Bingen said, have I ever experienced myself as "a feather on the breath of God"? Can I characterize myself as being an open person? To what or whom am I most open? To what or whom am I often closed? Is vulnerability a virtue I seek to nurture and nourish in my life? In what ways am I prone to flee from my own or another's vulnerability? In free-flowing uncensored writing, record your responses. When finished, simply end without rereading anything you have written at this time.

Having gathered yourself into a focused place of reflection on expectancy, openness, and vulnerability, claim the quiet interior space where you sense openness to reconnect with the particular pathos of your unique personal history or present. Recalling the story of Ignatius's conversion (p. 2), remember that serious wounding is often a threshold to a greater depth of your interior life. You may choose to prepare for this meditation by listening to some instrumental music or track 12 of the CD, gazing into your garden, or walking meditatively before opening your journal. Take sufficient time to create a clear path into your inner atmosphere.

When you feel ready, begin to turn over the soil in this particular garden of memories. Go wherever your reflection on suffering takes you. Allow memories and images to surface without suppressing or judging them. Objectively and in an observing way explore periods of suffering in your life. As descriptive words surface that capture something of your experience of suffering, record them as they announce themselves to you, in you. Arising now from the contents of your own life these words begin to form a mantra.

Play with the words. Listen for the flow or melody of them, such as, "healing wounds abound" or "healing waters cleanse." All mantras are deeply personal and when they authentically announce themselves in us, they have a healing effect upon us, like a balm for the soul. Sister Joyce Kemp, r.c., shares the insight that mantras are a compression of words that hold seeds of the future. In their fluidity mantras move us forward by making a path for us to travel. In this mantra meditation your words form a bridge from pain to promise, from past to future.

Let the words flow that come from the wounded heart of your own experience.

Without self-censure or negative judgment, play with the words; work with the words to make the mantras that are true for you now.

Remember that working with memories of *pathos* may be wrought with frustration, unfinished business, and considerable sadness. It is important to accept that such past memories are part of the whole of you, belong to you, and actually contain hidden treasures buried in the rubble. Date your entry.

> Even a happy life cannot be without a measure of darkness
> and the word happiness would lose its meaning
> if it were not balanced by sadness.
> —C. G. Jung

> There are three words that provide keys to living our spiritual
> lives in the proper fashion:
> expectancy
> openness
> vulnerability.
> —Irene Dugan, r.c.

The nineteenth-century German philosopher Friedrich Nietzsche believed that the most spiritual human beings also experience by far the most painful tragedies, but it is precisely for this reason that they honor life because it brings against them its most formidable weapons. Coming into greater spiritual maturity is recognized by one's increasing capacity to embrace the paradox of *pathos*. Those events, situations, places, and people that were experienced as bringing the most darkness and threat of destruction remarkably became a birth canal for who you are today. Looking back now, can you see a pattern forming the coherent whole of your life?

We can refer to this kind of meditation as working with the past in order to recover vital elements of your spiritual, interior history. Your immersion into your own *pathos* is part of cleaning up your inner atmosphere, entering into your storehouse of memories, giving yourself permission to claim and articulate your perceptions of what happened and how you once felt and feel today in retrospect. The mantras are a gift from that time into your present life. From a depth psychological perspective, what you are striving to describe is the process of individuation or self-realization: the particular way of your particular journey to wholeness and integrity. Our unique characters and personalities are most authentically forged through our experience of suffering. This is not to demean our accomplishments and joys in living, but growth is most expansive through emotional and spiritual pain, a situation that defies a completely rational explanation. There is a regressive pull in each of us to give up and quit the business of individuation, to escape the painful human process of becoming a distinct, separate, fully alive personality (Johnson 1998, p. 192). Such are the challenges of the journey toward spiritual salvation – wholeness and holiness – that will inevitably lead one to the garden of *pathos*, ripe with betrayal and potential.

The mantras you have just recorded are brimming with insight into your spiritual future. Conclude this period of meditation and journal entries by receiving the words of the prophet Jeremiah (track 13):

> *For I know the plans I have for you, says the Lord,*
> *plans for your welfare and not for evil,*
> *to give you a future and a hope.*
> *Then you will call upon me*
> *and come and pray to me,*
> *and I will hear you.*
> *You will seek me and find me;*
> *when you seek me with all your heart,*
> *I will be found by you, says the Lord.*
>
> (Jer. 29:11–14a NRSV)

The Last Supper

The preceding exercise is a cleaning up of the inner atmosphere in preparation for Ignatian contemplation on the passion of Jesus, who is, for the Christian, the paradigm of human becoming. Ignatius opens the third week with contemplation on the final meal Jesus shared with his friends.

Paintings of the Last Supper are numerous and diverse. Many Christian homes and nearly every refectory or dining room in a Catholic religious community has a copy of one of the masters' portrayals of the event in evidence. Yet, I am led to wonder, along with Ignatius, how much thought is given to contemplating all the historic and symbolic meaning of this great story of faith and freedom.

Jesus and his apostles were celebrating an ancient ritual on that sacred eve. They and all the Jews were remembering a historical event: freedom from slavery to the Egyptians eons before. The Book of Exodus chronicles this amazing story, which is celebrated by Jews everywhere each year generation upon generation (Exod. 12–15). Passover was the name given to this event because the Angel of Death passed over the dwellings of the Jews whose doorjambs were marked with the blood of a lamb. Origins of this sacred meal in the practices of pastoral or nomadic conditions of life have age-old significance in the history of Judaism. It was a spring rite to insure the successful movement of the nomadic clan and the flock to summer pastures. The Israelites reinterpreted this in terms of the Exodus. The Passover meal was sacred protection for their movement away from slavery. The first Passover meal marked the end of an era.

Yahweh tried various means, with Moses as ambassador, 'o press the Egyptians to free the Israelites. Pharaoh refused to let God's people go even amid the onslaught of plagues aimed at revealing Yahweh's power (Exod. 8–11). It was the final plague that gave birth to the Passover. "And Moses said, 'Thus says Yahweh: about midnight I will go forth in the midst of Egypt; and all the first-born in the Land of Egypt shall die, from the first-born of Pharaoh, even to the first-born of the maidservant . . . and there shall be a great cry throughout all the land of Egypt, such as there has never been, nor ever shall be again" (Exod. 11:4–6). The Israelites were saved only if they followed the ritual commanded by Yahweh. Each family was to slaughter and roast a year-old lamb or kid and eat it with unleavened bread and bitter herbs. "In this manner shall you eat it: your loins girded, your sandals on your feet, and your staff in hand; and you shall eat it in haste. It is Yahweh's passover" (Exod. 12:11). They were to daub their doorposts with the blood of the lamb so that the Angel of Death would know to pass over their homes (Exod. 12:7). It was freedom from slavery and death. It was their ritual meal of exodus, literally meaning, "to be led forth."

The ancients had a different awareness of the relation of blood to life than we do today. Our North American ability to replace lost blood with transfusions or plasma has erased from modern consciousness the urgency and sacrality of the blood-life connection. We save our own blood weeks before surgery should we need it during the operation. We run blood drives in order to keep the blood banks stocked for emergencies. We expect that if we need blood we will get it and thus preserve life. Only rarely is there great anxiety regarding the availability of blood. Only rarely do we rise up to protest the needless shedding of blood, often perpetrated in one of God's names, in the hundred or so religious wars being fought daily on our planet as you read this page. We fail to savor the religious symbolism of blood as the flow of life itself. If we did, we could not live as we are living.

Literary and biblical scholar and author Thomas Cahill explores the ancient story of the Lindow Man, who reveals yet another example of the religious symbolism of blood and life, sacrifice and saving. Cahill reports that the Lindow Man was a Druid prince striving to protect Druidism from Roman control around 60 C.E. He offered himself as a sacrifice to the gods for the defeat of the Romans. Cahill says,

> The digestive tracts of all these sacrificial victims have been analyzed to see what their last meal might tell us about their circumstances . . . [The Lindow Man's] esophagus was found to contain only some bits of blackened hearthcake, a rather odd last meal. [British archaeologists] Anne Ross and Don Robins rightly remind us that a scorched or blackened piece of unleavened bread has long served in Celtic communities as a sign of victimhood . . . The most conclusive evidence that the bogmen were sacrificed is the story their bodies tell of the manner of their deaths. Each submitted himself naked to an elaborate, ritualized Triple Death. In the case of the Lindow Man, for instance, his skull was flattened by three blows of an ax, his throat garroted by a thrice-knotted sinew cord, his blood emptied quickly through the precise cutting of his jugular. Here is the ancient victim of sacrifice, the offering made out of deep human need.

Unblemished, raised to die, possibly first-born, set aside, gift to
the god, food of the god, balm for the people, purification, repa-
ration for all – for sins known and unknown, intended and inad-
vertent. Behold god's lamb; behold him who takes away the sins
of all. (Cahill 1995, pp. 138–140)

This ancient Druid story expands our consciousness to appreciate the transcultural, dare we say cosmic, primordial meaning of
the gift of blood in response to deep human need. Moses and the
Exodus, Jesus and his Passion, the Lindow Man and his blood sacrifice, are archetypal. This means that the motifs of blood, sacrifice, and life are irrepressibly linked and will manifest over and
over again. As we become more conscious, we live aware of our
deep connections to the past, whose stories course through our
veins like blood.

Jesus carried the memory of the Exodus story of his people, felt
kinship with Moses, and dutifully celebrated the Passover meal
each year of his life. His final Passover – the Last Supper – inaugurates the passion of Jesus. He knew his hour had come and that his
mission would cost him his blood and his life. Christian scriptures
record that on the night when Jesus was betrayed, he took bread,
gave thanks, broke it, and said, "This is my body which is given up
for you. Do this in remembrance of me." At the conclusion of the
meal, Jesus took the cup, saying, "This cup is the new covenant in
my blood. Drink this in remembrance of me" (1 Cor. 11: 23–26;
Matt. 26:26–29; Mark 14:22–25; Luke 22:14–20). We find in Paul's
letter to the church at Philippi an enigmatic poem about sacrifice,
which is the oldest recorded Christian hymn:

Who, though he was in the form of God,
he did not count equality with God
a thing to be grasped,

but emptied himself,
taking on the form of a slave,
being born in the likeness of human beings.

And being found in human form
humbled himself and
became obedient unto death,
even death on a cross.

Therefore, God has highly exalted him
and bestowed on him the name
which is above every name,

that at the name of Jesus
every knee should bow
in heaven and on earth
and under the earth,

and every tongue confess
that Jesus Christ is Lord,
to the glory of God…

  (Phil. 2:6–11 NAB)

Christians believe that Jesus poured out his blood; gave his life in fulfillment of his promise: "I have come that you may have life and have it abundantly" (John 10:10).

The redemptive sacrifice of animals and humans came to an end with the Jesus of the gospels and the Christ of Christian faith. After recounting the story of the Lindow Man and St. Patrick's evangelizing mission to proclaim Jesus as a new Lindow Man, Cahill goes on to say:

> Yes, the Irish would have said, here is a story [the Jesus story] that answers our deepest needs – and answers them in a way so good that we could never even have dared dream of it. We can put away our knives and abandon our altars. These are no longer required. The God of the Three Faces has given us his own Son, and we are washed clean in the blood of this lamb. God does not hate us; he loves us. Greater love than this no man has than he should lay down his life for his friends. That is what God's Word, made flesh, did for us. From now on, we are all sacrifices – but without the

shedding of blood. It is our lives, not our deaths that this God wants. But we *are* to be sacrifices, for Paul adds to the hymn this advice to all: "Let this [same] mind be in you, which was also in Christ Jesus" (Phil. 2:5). (1995, pp. 141–142)

In the sixteenth century, Ignatius did not have the benefits of biblical historical, literary or textual criticism, or the insights of Jungian depth psychology, but he certainly grasped the importance of entering the fullness of the story of Jesus' Last Supper as a necessary threshold to an affective understanding of his and our passion.

Contemplation on the Passion

Choose an image, painting, sculpture, or some artistic expression of the Last Supper, taking time if necessary to find one prior to engaging in this contemplation. The scope of artistic renderings of this biblical scene is vast, from classic European artists, such as Leonardo da Vinci's masterpiece, to Latin American folk art influenced by liberation theology to depictions of the Last Supper that include women at the table.[1] It is worth the effort to consider a variety of images and find one that appeals to you and draws you into it.

Select a setting that includes a favorite table and chair and take your place. Prepare to enter a period of contemplation. You may choose to light a candle ceremonially and have a basket of unleavened bread and a cup of wine. Contemplation is an activity of the imagination in which you free your creativity to transport you from this table to the table of the Last Supper, the Passover meal, prelude to the *pathos* of the garden of suffering and sacrifice.

Read one of the accounts of the Last Supper from the synoptic gospels: Matthew 26:1–2, 14–16, 17–35; Mark 14:1–2, 10–11, 12–26; or Luke 22:1–39. John's gospel does not contain material on the Last Supper. John substitutes the breaking of the bread and sharing the cup with the action of Jesus washing the feet of his disciples. This is John's rendition of the meaning of the Eucharist. Reading John 13 will add additional images to your contemplation. You may want to add a visual image of this biblical scene or place a basin of water and a towel near the bread and cup on the table.

As you prayerfully read the following guided meditation, allow it to become contemplation by occasionally pausing, closing your eyes, visualizing the scene, and allowing your imagination to roam freely. At any time during the meditation, stop to note in your journal any feelings, thoughts, or insights that seem important to you.

Nourishment of every kind fills the room of the Last Supper, but we will pass by it for a moment to enter the atmosphere of the supper room. The meal is intended to be celebratory; however, the room is heavy with foreboding and urgency. Jesus is full of emotion, which brings forth feelings in his table companions. The washing of the feet calls forth an outburst from one of the twelve and then acquiescence. Jesus is concentrating on his impending death while at the same time dropping a bombshell about betrayal by one of the twelve and denial by another. Communion is being given through bread broken and cup shared, through weary feet caressed and washed clean, and then taken away by impending death. No wonder the room is filled with confusion and uncertainty. No one could filter all that is happening. Add the solemnity of the Passover and its ritual eating and drinking; anything could happen, and it did.

No wonder later they will all fall asleep. They are drained, exhausted by the unspoken fears and cryptic implications of Jesus' strange words at a familiar meal.

And yet there is a heightened sense of the night's importance as there would be at any farewell meal. They recline with each other at table, praise God's name, eat and drink because it is their custom. Nourishment is experienced at its best that night. The verb "to nourish" carries the meaning "to flow," as in milk from a mother's breast. Only life can nourish life. Only life given freely in love can elicit life from others, who in turn give it away to others. "Do you understand," he said, "what I have done to you? You call me Teacher and Lord, and rightly; so I am. If I, then, your Lord and Teacher, have washed your

feet, you should wash each other's feet. I have given you
an example, that you also should do as I have done to
you" (John 13:12–15).

The bread that we broke was more than bread. The wine that we
shared was more than wine.

—Madeleine L'Engle

(from *Two-Part Invention: The Story of a Marriage,* p. 68)

Make a journal entry. Date your entry. If possible and with journal in
hand, go for a walk to a garden or visit a conservatory and sit for a time
watching and listening, outer and inner senses alert, to the creativity
and flow of life, abundant, sometimes in disguise.

Notes

1. Consider artist Bohdan Piasecki's "The Last Supper," in which women and
children are present (poster distributed by Avoca Publishers, Saint Francois, 26
Avoca Avenue, Blackrock, County Dublin, Ireland, www.newlastsupper.com),
or Mary Lynn Sheetz's "Women's Work," a Last Supper image with figures that
include Dorothy Day, Thea Bowman, Ida Ford, and Catherine of Siena (available from Sheetz, 25 West Las Vegas Street, Colorado Springs, Colorado 80903,
phone [800] 457-2302, www.alterni_ts.com).

7. Presence

✳

When the Lord has given you the bread of suffering and the water of distress, the one who is your teacher will hide no longer, and you will see your teacher with your own eyes. Whether you turn to right or left, your ears will hear these words behind you, "This is the way, follow it."

Isaiah 30:20–21(NJB)

Introduction

IF YOU HAVE TRAVELED THIS FAR INTO THIS BOOK, YOU ARE MOST likely aware that most people do not consciously seek spirituality in depth. This is a simple statement of observable fact and not an indictment. Most people find the challenges of daily living quite enough, thank you. Many of us have been mysteriously attracted to the personalities and proclamations of the great prophets of religious history, Jesus of Nazareth, the mystics, sixteenth-century Ignatius of Loyola, twentieth-century Carl Gustav Jung or Ira Progoff, or the many more modern voices that speak to exploring the terrain of our inner world and its workings.

In our journey thus far into deeper spiritual realms we are aware that the sabbath time given to develop inner senses and interior muscles begins to feel quite natural. Actually, the whole of this book is about a "natural spirituality."[1] At this point in the Ignatian spiritual path – the fourth week of Ignatius's Spiritual Exercises, into which we have integrated some of Progoff's insights – the spiritual journeyer has become supple within and ready to trust the prophet's promise. The bread of our suffering and the water of our distress are now experienced as the guise of the wise *rabbuni*. In John's gospel, Mary of Magdala returns to the tomb, finds it empty, and is conversing with a gardener when, in an instant of consciousness, she realizes the gardener is Jesus risen. Spontaneously, she speaks in Hebrew the name of recognition, "*rabbuni* – which means teacher" (Jn. 20:16). As Isaiah prophesized, the time comes when the teacher's presence is recognized as strikingly as the biblical cloud by day and pillar of fire by night and heard with unmistaken clarity, "this is the way, follow it." It is now possible to enter an interior condition of presence.

> *For this is what Divine Spirit means: God present to our spirit. Spirit is not a mysterious substance; it is not a part of God. It is God . . . God as present in communities and personalities, grasping them, inspiring them, and transforming them.*
> —Paul Tillich
> (from *The Eternal Now*, p. 84)

What does it mean to be present? Nearly all the great spiritual traditions testify to the reality and power of presence. Presence is the intimation of transcendence in the ordinary or apparently mundane in life. Depth psychology refers to this phenomenon as synchronicity. More will be said of this later; for now, it is enough to say that synchronicity means one can see, feel, hear, taste, and touch the presence of the divine disclosed in the midst of daily living. In short, synchronicity is about very meaningful coincidences. True to the title of this book, we say that the transcendent is often in the disguise of the immanent and ordinary. Among all God's creations, humans are unique in possessing the capacity to interpret an epiphany: the inbreaking of the holy into any given moment. What gives the experience a christic dimension for Christians is the sense of personal relationship with the spirit of the risen Christ. It was very early "on the first day of the week" that the Christian scriptures testify to the encounter with the more than empty tomb, to the resurrection of Jesus from the dead (Matt. 28:1–20; Mk. 16:1–20; Lk. 24:1–53; Jn. 20:1–31).

This action ascribed to God's covenantal love signifies yet again the interpenetration of all matter with spirit. The human body is ensouled and carries within its physicality the very eternity of God, a presence powerful enough to sustain even the physical cessation of life. Even death cannot contain the spirit. There is a life that only lives by dying. And dying, as we know, is something we do many times, not once. The Christian mysteries of Resurrection, Ascension, and Pentecost are about the eternity we carry in our beings and the legacy we leave in perpetuity.

Presence collapses the barriers of temporality into an experience of mystical connections born of an awakened consciousness and the practice of contemplation. Sometimes the experience of presence announces itself synchronistically, arrives on its own accord and with its own energy. At other times, a developed memory has the power to invoke and provoke presence not immediately available to us in the physical sphere. This means a developed memory gives us access to or pulls up and out from our unconscious the sacred fragments of our story. Relying on the Ignatian invitations of the fourth week and the insights of depth psychology, this chapter explores how the Christian belief in the resurrection of Christ provides a framework or frame of reference to understand our own limitless possibilities for life in the Spirit. The chapter concludes with a series of guided contemplations based on Ignatius's directions for the fourth week.

Resurrection: Awakened to Infinity

Resurrection signifies a new mode of being. It is not the resuscitation of one's previous life but entry into new life never before experienced. Resurrection in Christian theology and spirituality includes notions of transformation, transfiguration, and recreation. The risen Christ transcends all the particularities and limitations of earthly existence and is transfigured as a new spiritual life form, a new creation. This is the reason why Mary of Magdala first thinks the risen Christ is a gardener and, in Luke's gospel, why the disciples on the road to Emmaus fail to recognize that the stranger walking with them is the risen Lord (Jn. 20:15; Lk. 24:15). To be transfigured is to be changed or altered in appearance; transformation is the extension of this process of *metanoia,* whereby one's essence and character become more vibrantly authentic and transparent. It is not uncommon to actually perceive someone looking different when they are engaged in a breakthrough period of life. Interior luster can manifest itself on the exterior and vice versa.

The Christian mysteries of the Resurrection, Ascension, and Pentecost complete the paschal mystery, the "passing over" of the earthly Jesus to new life in God as the Christ who resides forever in our midst as Spirit, Way, Truth, and Life. This is a life, a way of living, which only come to life by dying . . . to something radically new. Theologian Karl Rahner describes the experience when he says,

> Thomas Aquinas is the mystic who adores the mystery, which is beyond all possibility of expression. Thomas is not of the opinion that because theology deals with the infinite mystery of God it may talk imprecisely or vaguely. But he is neither of the opinion that the precise language of theology should give the impression that we have discovered the secret and caught the mystery of God in the subtle nets of theological concepts. Thomas knows that the highest precision and sober objectivity of *true theology ultimately serves one purpose: to force the individual out of the lucid clarity of his [her] existence into the mystery of God, where he [she] no longer grasps but is moved, where he [she] no longer reasons but adores, where he [she] does not master but is overpowered.* (Rahner 1996, p. 317, emphasis added)

This is indeed the mood and tone entering the fourth week of the Ignatian Exercises. Ignatius invites meditation and contemplation on the Resurrection as having less to do with the next life and more to do with the new life abundantly surrounding us in the now of our lives. We can live in the pervasive mysterious presence of the God of life, where we no longer grasp but are moved, no longer mercilessly insist on reasonableness but quietly adore, and where we are freed from the need to control and experience being overpowered by Presence.

Formidable resistance often accompanies the arrival at any new threshold to the next doorway of growth. Entry into the experience of resurrection, being awakened to our infinity, is an experience we desire but fear will never happen to us. Resurrection is an experience of a deeper separation than we have ever experienced. The thought of it can distress more than elate us. We know we have a direction to follow: the attainment of finishing our work. We may feel it will be a perilous direction to enter, but it will not be half as perilous as being completely out of sync and adrift in seas of doubt and fear that are paralyzing. We are content with what is familiar and known; and, consequently, hang on to it with great tenacity. There is a genuine suffering in the conscious sacrifice of the familiar. Our old complacent ego-driven consciousness fears death but it must so die in order to be superceded by a new level of consciousness. This is the natural path of individuation; while indeed the narrow way, it is the one that leads to life.

For Christians, Jesus is the only experienced source of our knowledge of this event. Thus, we rely on his story to shape and ignite our imaginations as to what such a new beginning could be for us. We know that his Resurrection signified a new mode of living. Christian scriptures record that after the Resurrection Jesus still bore the marks of his suffering. These are the sacred wounds, which become the seedbed, source, and wellspring of a new life. Such wounds glow with vitality and bleed forth healing. His wounds are transfigured and transforming. Jesus ran his course, finished his work, and was raised to *new life* by *Abba* for the completion of a life given in love. This is why the Jesus of Nazareth – the Jesus of history – became the Christ of faith at the Resurrection.

Christ appeared to those ready to see him and to those who were skeptical as a proof of his word that he would die and, on the third day, rise to new life. The women and disciples witnessed the fact of the Resurrection through their encounter with the presence of the risen Christ. It took considerable time for those in the Cenacle to receive the presence of Christ as real, to accept the possibility of an expanded reality, which included resurrection (Mt. 28:17–18; Mk. 16:14–15; Lk: 24:10–11). No doubt the word of the witnessing women was untenable to them, since the culture of the time prohibited women's word to count as trustworthy testimony.[2] Their fear was simply too great to leave room for the possibility that Jesus had truly risen, alive in some new way. There must have been some subtle jostling for power, some competition among them as to who would break the silence of their hiding in the upper room.

The style of the risen Christ offers an interesting counterpoint to the apostles and disciples. There is an amazing simplicity in how the gospel authors record the post-resurrection sequences. Jesus as the Risen One simply appears on the scene, his tone and manner invitational, not confrontational. The gospels record the risen Christ as saying, "Look at me . . . touch me"; "Peace"; "Do not be afraid"; "Go out, confirm the word by the signs you do"; "You will be clothed with power from on high"; "I will send the Spirit to you"; "Receive the Holy Spirit"; "I send you forth . . . teach, make disciples"; and the poignant and powerful last verse of the Gospel of Matthew, "And know that I am with you always; yes, to the end of time" (Mt. 28:20).

We do well to consider the words of the British poet Christopher Logue, who captures an image of the struggle to trust resurrection's edge:

> *Come to the edge.*
> *We might fall.*
> *Come to the edge.*
> *It's too high!*
> COME TO THE EDGE!
> *And they came,*
> *and he pushed,*
> *and they flew.*
>
> (from *Selected Poems*, p. 64)

The Gift of Presence

Those closest to Jesus could not bear the thought of life without him in the flesh. They were on the threshold of something new and stood paralyzed by his ignominious death and perilously close to the edge of what their collective consciousness could hold. While in their company Jesus made promises of remaining with them in some new way. Their minds were too cluttered with fears and their senses dull to the truth he attempted to communicate in word, symbol, and action. Jesus revealed that presence transcends what can be immediately grasped. One of the lessons he taught is that presence is an essential dimension in relationship. The bread broken at supper is more than bread; the cup shared among friends is more than wine.

It is an irony that after millennia of being shaped by this story we fail to experience the tangible in the mystical and equate presence exclusively with the physical world.

> Desire is, in essence, infinite, but its objects are always finite. Troilus says to Cressida, "This is the monstrosity in love, Lady, that will is infinite, the execution confined, the desire boundless, the act a slave to limit." But experience over a lifetime reveals a pattern of changing and deepening desire, in which I begin to realize, through a succession of deaths, what I – the true self – want, which is infinite. Life is desire slowly becoming itself. Life is the progressive liberation of desire . . . .
>
> Still, this desire, while feeling its infinity, was necessarily channeled into the finite Jesus, its awakener. At the climax of the story, the channel is destroyed, to produce a death of ego in which every thing is lost. With the Risen Jesus, desire infinite in its essence becomes infinite in its exercise. Desire is liberated, becomes itself. This is why the Risen One is invisible, partakes of the invisibility of God known in the Spirit. Resurrection is the liberator of desire. (Moore 1990–91, pp. 496–97)

The human hand cannot touch much of what we hold precious. Love, for example, can never be coerced but when it is freely offered its presence warms our heart and makes it beat faster. We gasp in awe at the panoramic beauty of nature as we feel we are enveloped into a scene of majesty beyond belief. Or, how does one hold truth in one's hand? Or integrity?

The word *presence* houses the word *essence.* Essence is our beingness, our sense of self and our unique gift. Our essence is our presence, and presence remains even in absence.[3] For our purposes, essence, spirit, and soul are inseparable terms. Gerald May says that a human being does not have a soul. A human being is a soul. With this understanding, we can take soul to mean the fundamental essence of a person, while the spirit is the aspect of that essence that gives it power, energy, motive, direction and force (May 1982, p. 32). The mystery about which we speak is not about re-experiencing the previously known; it is about a *new* experience of a *new* way of relating as beings-in-the-world. The Resurrection of Jesus provides a framework by which we come to know, as Rahner says, the objective reality of Incomprehensible Mystery, where we no longer grasp after but are moved inwardly; no longer idolize the rational but permit ourselves the pleasure of adoring; where we release our control and remain open to be overpowered by a Great Awakening.

Learning to live in presence always includes a sense of mission that presses one beyond the self. Our vocation is always about our life work on behalf of the transformation of the world in the direction of God's reign of justice and shalom.[4] The inner journey is about the balance of self-discovery with our call toward reconciliation with those with whom we make our life and with whom we share our world. From a Christian perspective, the goal of the sending forth of the Spirit is no less than to renew the face of the earth. The energy of the Spirit prods us in the direction of a love that requires the embrace of self, Self, and other. We have only to let this vision filter through us to the marrow of our bone in order to be transformed by the enduring presence of Jesus in Spirit. Zeal for the realization of the resurrected life here and now burns out the consuming self-centered preoccupations and ignites a larger vision. In essence, ancient wisdom from the Hebrew Scriptures, the Shema, and an enduring gospel mandate brings us back to the beginning of this chapter. The prophet Isaiah foretells that the time comes when the teacher hides no more. Senses are awakened to hear, "This is the way, follow it":

Court her with all your soul,
and with all your might keep her in your ways;
go after her and seek her; she will reveal herself to you;
once you hold her, do not let go.
For in the end you will find rest in her
and she will take the form of joy for you.

(Ecclesiasticus 6:26–28 NJB)

Hear, O Israel, The Lord your God is one. You shall love Yahweh, your God, with all you heart, with all you soul, with all your strength. Let these words I urge on you today be written on your heart . . . teach them to your children . . . write them on the doorposts of your house and on your gates. (Deuteronomy 6:4–9 REB)

You must love the Lord you God with all your heart, with all your soul, with all your mind. This is the greatest and first commandment. The second resembles it: You must love your neighbor as yourself. (Matthew 22:38–40 NJB)

The key to living new life in the present is found paradoxically in the permanently meaningful truth of very old words.

True theology ultimately serves one purpose:
to force individuals out of the lucid clarity of their
existence into the mystery of God,
where they no longer grasp but are moved,
where they no longer reason but adore,
where they seek not mastery but yield to being overpowered.

—Karl Rahner, SJ
(adapted from *The Great Church Year*, p. 317)

A Fourth-Week Contemplation

We turn our attention to integrative experiences that personalize and deepen the insights into the risen life proposed in this chapter. As mentioned earlier, an understanding of Jung's notion of synchronicity is valuable for engaging in contemplation of the symbolic meanings of the resurrection.

Synchronicity helps explain the phenomena of those moments of awareness when the outer world and the inner world spontaneously link.[5] Formally, Jung defined synchronicity as an acausal connecting principle present in nature. "Through it," Hudson notes, "events in life are linked not by physical cause and effect but by meaning arising from the unconscious" (2000, p. 104). Hudson goes on to say:

> There is, for example, an answer to the demands on our time, a way through the hours of the day. Synchronicity gives us hints. The elevator that is too full directs us to the stairwell where we meet the person we need to see ... Through synchronicity the unexpected check comes in the mail just in time to cover the unexpected dental expenses... A friend happens to call just at the time we are beginning to sink into an emotional quagmire ... Through synchronicity we learn that life has its own wisdom, much greater than our own, and that to avail ourselves of it, we must be constantly aware and alert ... And although synchronicity does not shield us from difficulty and pain, it brings mercy into our dark times in the way events unfold ... Attunement to synchronicity makes us artists of life, conscious participants in God's creative spirit. (Ibid., p. 108)

Fleming, in his translation of the Spiritual Exercises, offers some modifications on entering the contemplations of the fourth week. His contribution is important in preparing for a contemplative period of reflection. He speaks in the first person:

> As soon as I awake, I recall the atmosphere of joy, which pervades this week, and review the particular mystery about which I am to contemplate. Throughout the day, I try to keep myself in

a mood, which is marked by happiness and spiritual joy. As a result, anything in my environment – the sun and warm weather or the white cover of snow, all the different beauties of nature, and so on – is used to reinforce the atmosphere of consolation. (1996, p. 173)

Fleming encourages an enthusiastic alertness and attunement to one's inner and outer environment. Begin to feel "in sync" with an atmosphere of joy and consolation. Open yourself to whatever is to happen.

Review pp. 19–21 or listen to tracks 4 and 5 on the CD. If possible, save this contemplation for early morning to correspond to the time of day that the discovery of the empty tomb and encounter with the Risen One took place. Imaginatively place yourself in a garden surrounded by huge boulders before proceeding to read the following passage:

It was very early on the first day of the week and still dark, when Mary of Magdala came to the tomb. She saw that the stone had been moved away from the tomb and came running to Simon Peter and the other disciple, the one Jesus loved. "They have taken him out of the tomb," she said, "and we don't know where they have put him."

So Peter set out with the other disciple to go to the tomb. They ran together, but the other disciple, running faster than Peter, reached the tomb first; he bent down and saw the linen cloths lying on the ground, but did not go in. Simon Peter who was following now came up, went right into the tomb, saw the linen cloths on the ground, and also the cloth that had been over his head; this was not with the linen cloths but rolled up in a place by itself. Then the other disciple who had reached the tomb first also went in; he saw and he believed. Till this moment they had failed to understand the teaching of scripture that he must rise from the dead. The disciples then went home again.

Meanwhile Mary stayed outside near the tomb, weeping. Then, still weeping, she stooped to look inside, and saw two angels in white sitting where the body of Jesus had been, one at the head, the other at the feet. They said, "Woman, why are you weeping?" "They have taken my Lord away," she replied, "and I don't know where they have put him." As she said this she turned round and saw Jesus standing there, although she did not recognize him. Jesus said, "Woman, why are you weeping? Who are you looking for?" Supposing him to be the gardener, she said, "Sir, if you have taken him away, tell me where you have put him, and I will go and remove him." Jesus said, "Mary!" She knew him then and said to him in Hebrew, "Rabbuni!" – which means Teacher. Jesus said to her, "Do not cling to me, because I have not yet ascended to my Father. But go and find the brothers, and tell them: I am ascending to my Father and your Father, to my God and your God." So Mary of Magdala went and told the disciples that she had seen the Lord and that he had said these things to her. (John 20:1–18 JB)

After the first reading of the text, attend to the thoughts, images, ideas, feelings, or bodily sensations that emerge. Without judgment or self-censoring, record what surfaces for you in your journal. Date your entry.

Now feel the desire to be part of this biblical scene. Ask for the desire to place yourself in this mystery. Using the gifts of your inner senses, transcend the burdens and temporality of this time and cross into the garden. Be Mary of Magdala.

I saw a man, the gardener he seemed to be. I said to him, "Show me where you have laid the Lord and I will take him away." Then, a familiar lyrical voice said my name, "Mary." It was . . . at first I didn't recognize . . . then, I saw him. "Rabbuni," I almost shouted. I reached for him and clung to him in joy beyond imagination. I wanted to hold him fast so he wouldn't disappear but he said, "Don't hold me, go now and tell the others." I ran.

So much is racing through my mind as I run . . .

Did this really just happen?

Maybe in my grief and confusion, I allowed the gardener to console me and when he called me by name I imagined Jesus to still be alive. I've done this before after a death . . . thought I heard or saw a beloved, and for an instant, imagined that death had not visited me.

Why wouldn't he let me hold onto him?

What will I say to the others? They will think me mad.

How do I know for sure that what I experienced was real?

In your journal record your responses in a free-flow writing style without embarrassment, judgment, or self-censure. After you are finished, reread the entry and note anything further that seems important to record. Date your entry.

Continue to hold yourself in this biblical scene. Ask for the desire to place yourself in this mystery. Using the gifts of your inner senses, transcend the burdens and temporality of this time and cross into the moment when Mary of Magdala finds Peter, and Peter sets off running to the empty tomb. Be Peter.

I'm running and trailing behind John. I'm so exhausted from all that has happened. I can hardly carry my body back to that place. I am such a fraud and failure. At least I can muster the courage to go inside the cave of death. I felt a presence but could see no one. In the presence I heard him say to me, "Peter, true repentance teaches great lessons about pride and arrogance. You are my friend and I love you." I melted and felt being held fast.

What really happened here? The tomb was empty. Death wrappings tossed about. Could mean anything. But, I knew he was there with me. I felt him all around. I heard his voice speak within me. I felt so sad about my failing him but the feeling passed so quickly and melted into a profound peace. Before John entered the tomb, I heard myself say aloud, "It's all true. He is risen. What now?"

If it is all true, what now?

In your journal record your responses in a free-flow writing style without embarrassment, judgment, or self-censure. After you are finished, reread your entry and note anything further that seems important to record. Date your entry.

Meditation with the Body

Since Christian faith holds that it was Jesus' *body* that was raised from the dead, once again underscoring the incarnational nature of Christianity and, at its truest depth, holding a profound respect for the human body, it seems only natural to include a meditation that fully engages the human body.

Both Progoff and Ignatius are sensitive to the significant role of our bodies in spiritual life and growth. Both represent the best in a holistic approach that sees the connections between nutrition, physical activity, and human well-being. Throughout the Spiritual Exercises we are invited to savor the bodily, to engage our bodiliness, to become spiritually intentional about normal activities, such as being more aware of our bodies just before we fall asleep, or when waking up, or dressing for the day. Walking. Standing. Lying down. Sitting. Kneeling.

> *Since both soul and body belong to your Creator . . .*
> *you should pursue every means to strengthen the body . . .*
> *with a healthy mind in a healthy body, the whole*
> *will be healthier and more apt for God's service.*
>
> —Ignatius in a letter to Francis Borgia, duke of Gandia
> (from *Letters of St. Ignatius of Loyola*, pp. 179–182)

A section entitled "Rules for Eating" appears in the Spiritual Exercises following the contemplation on the Last Supper (see Fleming 1996, pp. 161–65).

Progoff reminds us that while much of the contents of our lives are expressed through our emotions, aspirations, and the activities of our inner world, our body *carries* them all. He says, "To that degree, our personal existence is dependent on our body. In a further sense, we make our contact with the world of nature, with music, the physical arts of dance and sports, sexuality and the realm of the senses all by means of our body" (1992, p. 154). Our body is the instrument of our most intimate relationships with self, other and the world. The body carries a natural wisdom.

A slogan for a running shoe synchronistically noticed not too long ago prompts the physicality of a fourth-week meditation-in-motion. A popular shoe manufacturer markets its product with this ad: *Marathoning – The Triumph of Desire Over Reason.* In the preceding scripture text we read of bodies-in-motion carrying a message beyond all reason. Mary, Peter, and John all *ran,* as if on fire, with a story to tell.

If you have the physical ability to run or "power-walk," embody the preceding contemplation. Make it contemplation-in-action. Choose to enter imaginatively into the character and essence of Mary, Peter, or John and set off on a run attending to the gift of your body bearing the capacity to be moved by desire. What is the message(s) you carry in your body that seeks expression? What is the story with which you are running?

After the run, record your responses in a free-flow writing style without embarrassment, judgment, or self-censure. After you are finished, reread your entry and note anything further that seems important to record. Date your entry.

If, however, you are limited in physical ability or, like me, confined to a wheelchair, imagine, as I do, that in the fullness of the risen life, you walk, even dance, freely. Enter contemplatively into the spiritual joy and consolation I found in the following vignette from David Adam's *The Cry of the Deer:*

> One cold grey day, I climbed up on to the high moors. The game-keepers were up there "burning off" the heather, and their fire attracted me. There was a great blaze. For a while I just enjoyed the warmth and companionship. The heather was perishing in the

flames; it hissed as it burned. These men knew what they were doing, all was planned and under control. The area for "burning off" had been chosen carefully. The heather here had become old and useless, all twisted and gnarled; it had lost its sweetness and no longer sustained the moorland life. So, it perished in the flames. The gamekeepers made sure the peaty soil did not burn. After the fire, the earth would be bare, blackened, lifeless. Then, one day, new shoots would begin to show. The heather had not been harmed and soon sweet, life-sustaining heather would grow once more. It had not perished, but would arise, phoenix-like, from the flames.

Here for me was a picture of the Resurrection: the old body may be destroyed; yet the essential being will not perish but have everlasting life. Watching the fire, I looked forward to the new green shoots. An old French tune came to mind and the words, "Love is come again":

In the grave they laid him, Love whom men had slain.
Thinking that never he would wake again.
Laid in the earth, like grain that sleeps unseen:
Love is come again
Like wheat that springeth green.

Forth he came at Easter, like the risen grain
He that for three days in the grave had lain.
Quick from the dead my risen Lord is seen:
Love is come again
Like wheat that springeth green.

When our hearts are wintry, grieving or in pain,
Thy touch can call us back to life again.
Fields of our hearts that dead and bare have been:
Love is come again
Like wheat that springeth green.

Leaving the gamekeepers and the "burning-off," I returned home strangely warmed, not by their fire, but by the Presence of the

Risen Lord. There on the moor He had come again, and for me the day was no longer dull and grey. (1987, pp. 47–48)

After a period of savoring this foray to the moors, record your responses in a free-flow writing style without embarrassment, judgment, or self-censure. After you are finished, reread your entry and note anything further that seems important to record. Date your entry.

In the next chapter, we explore love, the transformer.

ED. NOTE: *The following journal entry was made by Sister Irene Dugan and found among her notes for this chapter. While Sister Dugan was adamant that journal entries remain private, the fact of her including this entry among her notes suggests her desire that it be included in her published work. Her entry is recorded here without editing or comment.*

June 22, 1996

Through the Resurrection/Ascension Jesus completed the work given him by the Father. All he had to do to assure the continuance of his work was to send the Spirit. The work of the Great Counsel (begun by the Trinity in the beginning of time) is the growing and fostering of life that will never end. Living on a wider more expansive scale, once awakened, will never cease pulsating.

Resurrection of the body conjures up a picture of a transformed body: one no longer susceptible to disease and death. A body of extraordinary light and beauty. No wonder the apostles couldn't believe their eyes. They had never witnessed the like. How could limited, earth-bound humans even imagine or hope for such transformation! Extraordinary, yes, however, once we begin to grasp a corner of the picture, we are enthralled by its truth and have to follow our star. Stargazers follow stars. Such is part of formation of our spirit.

> *Stargazers follow stars.*
> —Irene Dugan, r.c.

Notes

1. A debt of gratitude is owed to author Joyce Rockwood Hudson in her work, *Natural Spirituality: Recovering the Wisdom Tradition in Christianity* (2000). Hudson defines natural spirituality as a human capacity to interpret the abundant manifestations of the Divine in creation and the ordinary events of one's life. Her work, rooted in the biblical creation traditions and based largely on Jungian psychology, suggests that the Spirit will naturally guide spiritual seekers on the quest for greater depths of self-realization. *Ed.*

2. The placement of Mary of Magdala as the first witness to the Resurrection is one of the instances in which all four gospels concur, and it is significant because women of the time were excluded legally from testifying. *Ed.*

3. For a rich description of spiritual absence, see Paul Tillich, "Spiritual Presence" (Tillich 1963).

4. For the story of Sister Dugan's final ministry among urban at-risk youths, see Bruce Wellems, CMF, "From Generation to Generation: Passing on the Legacy of Hope" (Clendenen 2002, pp. 139–147).

5. Murray Stein provides an experience of synchronicity related to Irene Dugan, r.c., in "Reality of the Soul" (Clendenen 2002, pp. 19–33).

8. Transformational Spirituality

Introduction

I GNATIUS CALLS THE FINAL CONTEMPLATION OF THE SPIRITUAL Exercise on the love of God "*Contemplatio Ad Amorem*," translated "Contemplation to Attain Love." In Spanish, the native language of Ignatius, it is "*Contemplacio para alcanzar Amor.*" Many threads of meaning can be spun from these few words. A poetic rendering of the phrase "*contemplacio para alcanzar amor*" suggests the dynamic notion of catching up with someone who keeps moving ahead. There is energy in this phrase. Ignatius is conveying the dynamics of spiritual presence as that which is moving ahead of us even as we are constantly moving toward it. In a sense, a more spiritually appropriate translation of Matthew's Gospel 5:7 reads: "Ask*ing*, you will receive, seek*ing*, you will find, knock*ing*, the door will be opened for you." Most often that phrase is translated as though it describes a single, once-and-for-all action, yet the intent is really a way of living. From my vantage point, love is the dynamic mystery of motion moving in us and through us as we are asking, seeking, knocking, attaining, yearning, hoping.

The human experience of love is a gathering together within the temple of our being all our energy and dynamism to apprehend Love. Love is the most needed, least understood and heeded of human necessities. Love is an unparalleled gift that is too often avoided, even discarded.

We speak of a "labor of love" or of "love's labor lost" with stress on the word *love* and pass over the prime word *labor*. Labor has the flavor of creating, preserving, and developing something, something we have inherently, and so is an incessant knocking for our attention and response. God does this to perfection, laboring over their handiwork. [1] We are invited and required to enter into their labor in order to shape ourselves under their tutelage, to their image. Through this mutuality, we take on the world, the cosmos, and love it to maturity.

And so we arrive at a deep attentive consciousness that knows "in my end is my beginning, and in my beginning is my end." Such unity is endlessly desired and so seldom entered into, because it is under our noses, and our noses have lost their sense of smell, due to inner and outer smog. Thus, the importance of cleaning up our inner atmosphere discussed in chapter 5. We need to come into our senses sharply and brightly so that we see freshly, hear acutely, touch tenderly, taste with relish, and take time to metaphorically and literally "smell the flowers."

> *[God] has showed you, O [humans] what is good;*
> *and what does the Lord require of you*
> *but to do justice, and to love kindness,*
> *and to walk humbly with your God?*
>
> (Micah 6:8 NRSV)

We are made sensuous beings and reclaiming this gift is an art to be cultivated, or we shall not be grasped by love. Love is a pure, sensuous gift, assuring me:

> I never was alone. I never am alone. I never will be alone, even if I disown the Presence. The automatic drive in me moves to constant self-awareness, self-alertness, self-development, and self-arrival. This faces me head-on to the Other, out of whom I spring, am shaped and formed, and a transforming union is experienced. This is my end and my beginning. (Buber 1996, p. 3)

In this day and age, my beingness and ability to come to Other spring from my daily experience of traveling through layers of accumulated artifacts of the self, to the cleansing waters and mirroring love of the Begetting Being.

Interaction of Lover and Beloved

Mutuality mediates transformation. Yet, transformation, as a process of growth, relies most often on the ordinary formative developments of our lives. The derivation of the word *transformation* comes from two Latin words, *trans* and *forma*. *Trans* literally means, "to cross over"; *forma* means "form, shape, figure, image, mold or stamp."[2] Transformation, then, is morphing, if you will, from one form to another. Formation begins in the womb of our mother, continues under family influence through infancy and early preschool years (though now, in the almost twenty-first century, due to the pressures of both parents working and the consequent explosion of child-care options, such family-based formation is not a given). The next stage of school, or its equivalent, makes a strong imprint on children. The experience of schooling has a definitive and defining impact on formation. This is followed in great intensity by entry into the demands of professional life and the many choices of avocations. We can be drugged by the lure of billboards, super sales techniques, and an unexamined grasping nature. We are shaped, reshaped, and misshaped through the unique features of our developmental process. At long last, if we are alive and alert, we begin to listen to our own life suggesting that it is time for us to take our formation into our own hands. This inaugurates a major transitional phase urging us to consider profound decision making about how we are going to live *now*.

Consciously examining the imprint of external authority on our lives, we gradually begin to take back the power over ourselves that we had given away and never acknowledged. The dumping/blaming syndrome comes to a grinding halt, as I am confronted with the self saying, "Now I begin . . . Begin? Begin what?" Re-formation! It is my turn to form, shape, and mold the product that is uniquely me according to the inner work at hand. A first question might be, "What is at hand?" Then follows the inventory of what it is at hand, meaning the native resources within myself, out of which I gradually create the SELF waiting to be born. Previously unobserved doors, windows, caverns, and heights emerge before me. Looking at them makes me shudder until I slowly quiet down and let my inner voice speaks, listening to love's lure and its direction. My life's journey shifts and the processes of mature transformation are summoned into reality. Transformation is a life-changing process that will result in dramatic, as well as evolutionary, reorganization of attitudes, behaviors, and meanings in life.

> *The energy of the central point is manifested in the almost irresistible compulsion and urge to become what one is.*
>
> —C. G. Jung
>
> (from "Concerning Mandala Symbolism," par. 634)

All creation has been awaiting this swell of the movement of love towards Love. This is indeed the summit of an Ignatian – a Christian – a human – spiritual vision. Transformation, as an endemic force in the press toward wholeness, while painful, demands an active giveover to love. The childish and adolescent exertions of egomania, fixations on what others think, and solely seeking external approvals loses its power and is replaced by an inner drive digging deeper into the essence of who I am and who I desire to be. Ah! This is conversion. The Psalmist sings, "Sacrifice and offering you do not desire; but you have given me ears that *dig after you*" (Psalm 40:6 NRSV). Reliance on the virtues of trust and fidelity create the inner condition that enables the journey to deeper regions of my being and taps the essential fundamentals of transformation. I become immune to the sirens of possession, hoarding, and, above all, success and its allurements. Wavering at this juncture of human becoming can spell disaster, serious wavering, that is, which carries the flavor of fearing the truth of spiritual adulthood.

The terrain is rugged, the riverbed not quite even, and so we fight and flow with the currents. Doubts that we are on the right way fly hither and thither in an attempt to erode trust and fidelity. Our beliefs are redefined from the inner out. The dross is burned away and the gold of love – the embrace of the sacrality and mutuality of our lives – begins to shine through. The moments when we are conscious of changing or having been changed are mighty moments. It is as if we *see* Love as a pillar of cloud by day and one of fire by night (Exodus 13:21–22 NRSV). The trust was worth the trusting; the faithfulness to the way, a journey to a promised land beyond our imagining. The state of transformation is rich with spiritual paradox: we live in an atmosphere of quietude and calm, and at the same time, of extraordinary activity surrounding the *kairos* of our becoming a new creation (II Corinthians 5:17 NRSV).

My will has now become supple and attentive to the voice of the Beloved, from whom I now hear the Voice within. At this level of intentional living and holy relationship, flexibility and fluidity of movement are reinforced. I am in union and harmony with Love. My whole being is infused with this awareness, and my desire is never to be separated from its passion.

> *THOU SHALT KNOW [GOD] WHEN [GOD] COMES*
> *Not by any din of drums –*
> *Not by the vantage of [any] airs –*
> *Not by anything [God] wears –*
> *Nor [any] gown –*
>
> *FOR [GOD'S] PRESENCE KNOWN SHALL BE*
> *By the Holy Harmony*
> *That [God's] coming makes in thee –*
>
> (Anon., fifteenth century)

Nestled in Holy Harmony is a mysteriously dynamic relationship. Transformation is mediated by this mutuality and has its entitlements and obligations, as any truly authentic and significant relationship. Life with the Beloved is strenuous because it involves living out the receiving and the giving of love. Attentive alertness to the Presence is imperative. Alert listening and hearing – activation of these inner senses – become second nature as the transforming process bears fruit. I live in tandem with creation and creativity; the music of the spheres envelops me, as I become a living God to the world, the universe, and the cosmos. A craving for simplicity in living and its consequent freedom reigns. Clinging to the old self ceases and falls away. I experience a sense of my inner environment as uncluttered and ordered. Love flows through me and neutralizes all disintegrative and destructive evil forces. Paul in his letter to the Galatians put it this way, "I live now not with my own life but with the life of Christ who lives in me" (Gal. 2:20 NJB). This is a season of alertness and inner brightness. Energy is neither blocked nor wasted. True life flows and is shared as love requires, and the lifeline is thus kept open for the free exchange, the giving and receiving of love. The process is simultaneously elevating and devastating.

> Rabbi Moshe Leib of Sassov said: "How to love [people] is some-
> thing I learned from a peasant who was sitting in an inn with other
> peasants, drinking. For a long time he was as silent as all the rest,
> but when he was moved by the wine, he asked one of the men seat-
> ed beside him: 'Tell me, do you love me or don't you love me?' The
> other replied: 'I love you very much.' But the first peasant replied:
> 'You say that you love me, but do you know what I need. If you real-
> ly loved me you would know.' The other had not a word to say to
> this, and the peasant who had put the question fell silent again. But
> I understood. To know the needs of men and women and to bear
> the burden of their sorrow – this is true love." (Buber 1996, p. 2)

Largesse Is Journey's End

Love opens our eyes, hearts, and hands in wide embrace of the all of life. An aura of eternity marks the season where largesse is Journey's End. The temporal has found its place and is the bridge to the other shore, also known as heaven. Heaven is an idea we tend to leave alone, bypass, or sigh over. We seem to fear swirling it around in a brandy snifter for taste, lest it evaporate, leaving us with nothing but the vapors. Yet, heaven does not ask us to address it, familiarize ourselves with it, so that we end up yearning for it with great inten-sity. For that to occur, we must devote time for savoring its mystery.

What do you feel, what do you think heaven to be like? St. Paul had this to say: "Of this wisdom it is written: Eye has not seen, ear has not heard, nor has it so much as dawned on [humans] what God has prepared for those who love [God]" (I Cor. 2:9 NAB).

When we are fully alive, alert, and aware here on earth, we are full of energy to explore, discover, and dig out every possible area of learning and experiencing the knowledge and wisdom at our fingertips. The excitement of increased knowledge and understanding through experience impels us into further searching, even when extra energy and push are necessary.

Heaven is going to be all this excitement, plus more, without the darkness and the disappointment that is inherent during our earthly pilgrimage. Boredom apparently is not a trait in God's being. Ergo, boredom ceases to exist in the largesse that is Journey's End. We will never live long enough to be satiated with respect to all the beauties and burdens of life. Music, science, literature, all areas of art, including culinary arts, are endless vistas open to our searching and inquisitive nature, to be pursued with pleasure, ease, and excitement. The challenges, enormous sorrows, and profound sufferings are but guises for growth. The God who stands by our side in times of struggle – always knowing our need and bearing our burden – is the same God who beckons us to the divine household at Journey's End where we reside forever in our natural dwelling place.

The gateway to this bliss is death, which turns out to be a friend rather than a foe. Death is the doorway of final transformation into unending life, light, and love. Death, then, as well as love, is the Transformer. Henri Nouwen writes,

> Dying is the most general human event, something we all have to do. But do we do it well? Is our death more than an unavoidable fate that we simply wish would not be? Can it somehow become an act of fulfillment, perhaps more human than any other act?
>
> . . . When we contemplate with compassion the suffering and pain both around the world and close to home, we receive a gift: a reminder of the great human sameness of all of us [who] will die and participate in the same end. When we offer companionship to the dying we remember and celebrate the lives of the departed, we create a reciprocal community of care and remind each other that we will bear fruit beyond the few years we have

to live. . . . When we face death with hope we make the choice of
faith, a choice based on the conviction that we see not only failure on the cross of Jesus, but victory as well, not only destruction, but new life as well, not only nakedness but glory as well.
(Nouwen 1994, p. xiv)

There is no satiety in heaven, only largesse. We experience the
wholeness of creation and our own as well, for all will be ours forever in freedom. Yet this experience is devoid of acquisitiveness to possess, dominate, or manipulate. All is healed, the human and divine
mingle and become one. In this dimension of new being there is no
need to believe because we shall have vision. We shall see God face-
to-face and bask in knowledge of the true Paternity/Maternity. Hope
will be absorbed in the final embrace of the God of our yearning.
What will remain is love – love as we never imagined could be experienced as real. The totality of living is ours in sheer wonder and joy.
Why, then, are we so shy about contemplating this reality?

Each of us will be transformed. Each of us will be a new creation and yet remain our true selves without impediments. We
will go to the depth of the sea and explore its treasures without
scuba diving equipment. We will fly to Uranus without space
ships. We will plumb the deep recesses of humanness, and our
largesse to embrace the discovery will be limitless. We will roam
with dinosaurs, understand and converse in all languages and no
language. We will sing arias and folk songs in praise of God. We
will experience what it actually means to be an heir of God. The
divine will shine in and through us, and it will be only the beginning. We shall be complete human beings in a continuing movement of union. The final awakening dawns in perpetual *amorem*.

When I dream of heaven, I experience a feeling of excitement
that what I am doing now is made more worthwhile by the vision
of what is to come. Therefore, it is the now that intimates what will
be. Therefore, I want to be related to and involved in the now of my
existence and not consumed by fear or searching for baubles and
commodities that erode and fade. I am the custodian of my soul
whose life is guided by the Master Crafter.

I am universal in that all that ever was exists in me. I am a song
of the Universe with all the chords of creation played out in me.

Such is the optimism of one who lives an examined life. Love is all around in the disguise of now.

The Now: Closing Meditations

Hopefully, the insights and exercises provided in this book have helped you plumb the greater depths of your own life, regain and reframe memories from the past, confront the shadow, befriend secrets, be less afraid of taking risks, and engage in creative imagining about the future. To maximize and consolidate a felt sense of integration, Progoff recommends taking time to "crystallize" your emerging vision of life, as well as claiming "hints" about the future often hidden in the disguise of the now of one's life. He refers to this kind of arrival as a "new now," the "open moment" of our life. Ignatian spirituality and holistic depth psychology are natural means through which we gain progressive inner perspective, enabling us to *feel from within* the movement of our life as it proceeds through its seasons of difficulty and accomplishment (Progoff 1992, p. 361). Progoff says that this effort, which he refers to as testament, is the fruit and flower of our interior practice. Expressing the very heart of the matter of our life vision is a personal "scripture being created from within us, out of the substance of our lives with the help of our commitment and our inner desire" (1992, p. 357).

> Begin this period of meditation by completing the calming and centering procedures that work best for you. If possible, you may want to listen to "Take, Lord, Receive," recorded by the St. Louis Jesuits or use Tom Kendzia's instrumental version as background music as you recite aloud the following prayer of St. Ignatius, which he includes in the contemplations of the fourth week.[3]

>> Take, Lord, receive all my liberty, my memory, my understanding, and my entire will – all that I have and call my own. You have given it all to me. To you, Lord, I return it. Everything is yours; do with it what you will. Give me only your love and your grace. That is enough for me. (Fleming 1996, p. 177)

Allow yourself to feel into the prayer and ask for the desire to place yourself – the whole of your life – at the disposal of God. Seek only to be in the presence of God's transforming love. That is enough. Repeat the prayer as often as necessary in order to make an effortless transition into meditation. Make a decision to honor what emerges without filtering or judgment. Place your journal nearby as you begin.

> *And the end of all our exploring*
> *Will be to arrive where we started*
> *And know the place for the first time.*
> —T. S. Eliot
> (from "Little Gidding," p. 145)

In this state of consciousness and openness to the spirit within and beyond yourself, reflect on the vision that guides your life. In the words of the prophet Habakkuk:

> *Write the vision down,*
> *inscribe it on tablets to be easily read.*
> *For the vision will have its appointed time,*
> *it hastens toward its end and it will not lie;*
> *although it may take some time, wait for it,*
> *for come it certainly will before too long.*
> (Habakkuk 2:2–3 NJB)

Jung reminds us that the future is always pushing up into our awareness and trying to get loose inside us so that we can hear it, see it, taste it, smell it, and touch it more clearly. The poet Rilke wrote that the future enters us long before it happens. Let the vision hasten forth. It need not be in prose. Words may come as poetry, in the form of a prayer, lyrics to music, or some other form of verbal expression.

Sit in stillness and in silence. Be poised to write. Trust the prophet's direction to "write the vision down." Record your vision in your journal as it emerges for you. Again, all that is necessary are a few lines that crystallize the heart of the matter. When you are finished *do not* reread or edit your testament. Simply close your journal and set it aside for a few days. Progoff says, "Even spiritual work has to be followed by a Sabbath!" (1992, p. 354). Date your entry.

Ignatian Recapitulation

After a period of Sabbath rest, you are invited to a concluding guided meditation.

Stein says, "The future is prepared in the womb of the past and the present" (Stein 1998, p. 16). Some people appear to have tumultuous discontinuities in life, but this, as we now know, is only a surface assessment. There is a thin thread that weaves continuously through the whole of our lives. We live in the mystery that all that we are and have been through personally and collectively has meaning and is part of our human and holy becoming.

> We begin this meditation with a recapitulation. This word is used here in a specific sense. For our purposes, a recapitulation includes a review or a recap of previous events, but it also includes another dimension. In spiritual recapitulation we return to the past for the purpose of discerning something new that is waiting to be discovered. In a sense, the past holds a key to the future, and in our backward glance we find a forward gaze; an open moment dawns before us. Our life follows a christic pattern – new life arises amidst the unlikely and thus often goes unrecognized.

> With a sense of inner and outer stillness, prepare to enter this experience of recapitulation. Open your journal and page through it from the beginning, stopping only long enough to remind yourself of all that has taken place on your spiritual journey. It is not necessary to study your writing. The goal in entering this meditation of recapitulation is to get a sense of the wholeness of the perspectives you have gained on your life, perspectives that have become, over time, more available to you, more real for you. While you have been working with the material in this book and making entries in your journal, new interior awakenings have been stirred to life, new insights born, greater balance felt, zest for living increased, and a vision of life more personally claimed. Close your eyes and gather the highs and lows, accomplishments and stumbling blocks, gifts and burdens of your spiritual journey.

Reread the vision you recorded in your journal in the previous meditation. Consider the future unfolding in the disguise of now. We return
to a question asked in the early pages of this book: Is the life I am living the same life that wants to live in me? You now can focus on that
question from the context of your life history as a whole. You stand
today on the threshold of a future nurtured in the womb of the past
and present. What direction is your life moving toward now?

In an atmosphere of silence, record responses to these questions in
whatever form captures what you seek to express. Let what you record
be a conscious recapitulation, a summary statement, a guiding image,
a stream of thoughts, a reminder of the thin thread of continuity, or a
hope. Whatever form it takes, record it as an expression of the energy
of the now, your opening to the future. Date your entry.

When you are finished, close your journal, hold it and extend it out
from you in a gesture of reverence for the all of your life and the potential waiting to be realized. You may choose to incense your journal, ring
a chime, and bow before the holy scriptures you have created in freedom and in truth.

Thus we draw this meditation to a close in peace.

Notes

The substance of this chapter appears under the title "Largesse Is Journey's
End" in *Spirituality in Depth: Essays in Honor of Sister Irene Dugan, r.c.*
(Clendenen 2002, pp. 6–17).

1. Sister Dugan understood God's dynamic nature as essentially Trinitarian. She
often made reference to Genesis 1:26, "Then God said, 'Let *us* make humankind
in *our* own image, after *our* likeness . . . .'" Plurality in God is critical to understanding fully the theological framework that informed Sister Dugan's lifework
in spiritual direction. The Christian doctrine of the Trinity, always mysteriously confounding, might be best expressed as one God with three ways of being:
(1) as Unconditional Love, *agape*; (2) incarnate and Incarnational, Word-made-
flesh; and (3) Life Source within the depth of each human spirit, Ground of
faith and hope, gifting each for others, Animator of community. In sum, we
experience God as one, yet as having three distinguishable ways of being. *Ed.*

2. For a more detailed etymology of *transformation*, see Stein 1998b, pp. 52–53. *Ed.*

3. *Let Heaven Rejoice: Music from the St. Louis Jesuits, Volume III* and *Come to
the Water: Instrumental Music, Volume III* by Tom Kendzia are available on
compact disc from Oregon Catholic Press.

9. The Feminine Divine

Editor's Introduction

It is a well-known tenet of depth psychology that human personality achieves its quest for wholeness and deep healing through the balancing of the features of masculinity and femininity within each human being. If wholeness is to be realized, albeit partially, then one must undergo the refining process of uncovering, discovering, and integrating the feminine and masculine dimensions – anima and animus *– of human personality.*

The anima *and the* animus *are the archetypal images of the eternal feminine and the eternal masculine, respectively. The anima is the feminine in a man's unconscious that forms a link between ego-consciousness and the collective unconscious and potentially opens the way to a more-integrated male self. The animus is the masculine in a woman's unconscious that forms the link that opens her to a more-integrated female self. While this type of thinking can easily lend itself to stereotyping, the essential notion of striving for deeper integration of the masculine and feminine in human personality is a worthy psychospiritual insight.*

A man develops his manhood not only by measuring up to the cultural standards of manliness or even archetypal feats of masculinity, but necessarily through a creative relatedness to the feminine, for without this embrace of the feminine within, masculinity becomes boorish and, at the extreme, brutal (Sanford 1984, p. 91). It is equally true that as a woman attempts to negotiate, adapt, and accommodate to the cultural expectations of her femalehood, even with archetypal feats of femininity, without the embrace of the masculine within, femininity falls prey to the weak-willed, manipulative, and depressive tyranny of the nice and kind.

As a student of Jung and friend of Ira Progoff, Sister Irene Dugan understood these insights and wove them into the art of spiritual direction she practiced with the women and men who sought her counsel. I vividly remember her sharing with me facets of her interesting relationship with Dr. Ira Progoff. Irene had had an encounter with Ira, who expressed to her that he thought she was a "very wise old woman and a very wise old man." At the time, Irene was nearly seventy, and I was in my late twenties. I knew that Ira had offered Irene an important gift in so naming her both a wise woman and a wise man. I knew that in sharing Ira's comment with me she was instructing me about the path of integration. I had a sense of the importance of this lesson, although I was far too young at the time to comprehend its wisdom.

In completing chapter 7, the four weeks of the Ignatian Exercises appeared finished, and I moved on to what I thought was the only remaining chapter in Irene's unfinished manuscript, the epilogue. To my surprise, I discovered a chapter simply entitled "The Woman." Clearly, Ignatius had no such theme in the flow of the Exercises. The chapter made only vague efforts to connect with Ignatian spirituality and offered only a single substantive reference to Progoff.

Trying to make sense of Irene's intention in developing this chapter, I eventually discovered a folder with various papers and in her handwriting read: "The Fifth Week: The Woman."[1] Thus, the wise old woman and wise old man, an Ignatian disciple for more than six decades, masterminds a fifth week to be added to the Spiritual Exercises of St. Ignatius! Feeling compelled to honor her effort, this chapter is included as a "fifth week" reflection. In this chapter, the reader will find Sister Dugan's original thoughts on creativity and sexuality, insights of importance for the religious imagination on Mary of Nazareth who became theotokos – Godbearer[2] – *and the wise meanderings of an old woman and old man who believed all things are possible with God.*

Most of our difficulties come from losing contact with our instincts, with the age-old unforgotten wisdom stored up inside us. And where do we make contact with this old man or woman in us? In our dreams.

—C. G. Jung, in McGuire and Hull, eds.,

C. G. Jung Speaking: Interviews and Encounters, p.89

Masculine and Feminine in God

IN THIS CHAPTER I WILL EXPLORE THE BIBLICAL FIGURE OF MARY and the Mary we have inherited through generations of Christian reflection upon her. What does it mean when the Christian Scriptures refer to Mary as "blessed among women"? The Church professes and re-professes Mary as singularly worthy, "full of grace"; litanies name her "mediatrix of all grace," "*Sancta Dei Genitrix*," co-redemptrix. Mary's choices underline that all women are copartners in God's activity of creating from the beginning.

We understand something very important about life with God by exploring Mary's way of being in relation to the God of her experience. In a strikingly singular way, this young woman of Nazareth revisits and revivifies the nature of the Creator God in the Book of Genesis:

> And God said:
>
> Let us make humankind [*'adam*] in our image, after our likeness .
> . . God created *'adam* in the image of God he created them; male and female God created them. (Gen. 1:26–27 NRSV)

While we know that our feeble attempts to grasp the nature of God are just that, nonetheless, the desire to know God prompts our hunger for deeper entry into God's mystery. Mystery is something about which there is always more to know. Mary lets us know something of God's intention in simultaneously fashioning from the earth creature, *'adam*, the sexual differentiation of maleness and femaleness – *is* and *issa* in Hebrew – precisely to more fully image the Creator God, within whom there is a fullness beyond the limits of gender. Masculinity and femininity commingle in God's own nature. So, we must conclude that male and female exist in God who is wholeness beyond what our meager language can convey.[3]

Human wholeness requires that these two aspects – masculinity and femininity – find reconciliation in each human personality. While we are each constituted, most often irreversibly, as either of the male or female sex, gender formation must strive for sympathy of connectedness. Our willingness to engage the making of a whole personality, not unlike Mary's willingness to engage God's offer, heightens our awareness that the feminine dimension in a man and the masculine dimension in a woman are essential parts of the whole. Each part brings a strand of color to the tapestry that is our unique life. The quality of the material figuratively depends on genes and chromosomes, but the durability depends on the time we invest in the weaving of our whole personality to mirror the Divine Intentionality in which we are created.

> In the sacred, sexuality and spirituality are integrated and draw vitality from each other.
> —C. G. Jung

Traditional theology and spirituality of the Trinity has not enjoyed the favor of the feminine as one of the life-giving dimensions of God's nature. The Trinitarian family seems to be a procession of maleness, each metaphysically begetting the next: Father, Son, and Holy Spirit. It stands to reason that there must be sexuality in God if *we* – human men and women – are mirrors of the abundance of God-life known as the Trinity. The mystery of sexuality has been avoided, dismissed, and demeaned long enough. It is time for us to approach all aspects of human experience, particularly sexuality, as sacred sources of life, invitations to almost limitless fruitfulness stamped in God's image and likeness. Rooted in this truth, the constant pregnancy of God is forever creating.

This said, we must consider what is involved in such a proposition. All creation is patterned on male/female principles. Each variety of life is continued by way of seed and fertilization; humans are no exception since we are seminal people. Seeds contain all the potential for new life, be it a carrot, a kitten, or a baby human. The giant redwood was once an infinitesimally small seedling. While we can scientifically explain these growth patterns, we will never exhaust the wonder that it actually happens in the endless cycles of birth, death, and rebirth, season upon season, generation upon generation.

God shares God's creative capacity with us so that each aspect of creation can re-create itself. God gives this divine capacity away to humans precisely so that we are not dependent but have initiative and ability to be relational and creative life-givers, in this regard, Godlike. The Book of Genesis records God's blessing human fruitfulness and God's sharing with *is* and *issa* the power to name and the responsibility to steward the creation given into human care (Gen. 1:28–31; Gen. 2:15, 19 NRSV). God is never diminished by these gratuitous acts. God is always about giving us to ourselves so that we thrive in the condition of being disposed to reciprocate freely in love, reverence, praise, and adoration. Such responses arise within us as a fundamental impulse, and in our freedom we actually possess the power to say "yes" or "no" to God (Rahner 1969a, pp. 206–210). This is an important point. If Mary (or Jesus) could not have said "no" to the call and mission, then her (and his) "yes" would have been stripped of its human value and meaning.

Images of Mary

The preceding has been a prelude to the place of woman within the scheme of reality charged with God's grandeur. God's choice to enter fully into the human experience required divine intimacy with one woman's "yes." There is no way into the human world except through woman. The historical woman of Nazareth is inescapably and inseparably intertwined with the mystery of the Incarnation. Mary is the bridge, the one among women, whose womb clothed and confected the body and blood of Jesus. The solemn blessing of the Christmas Vigil liturgy says, "When the Word became flesh, earth was joined to heaven."

There are but a handful of New Testament passages that open up for us a window on Mary. While Mary and Jesus are historically verifiable, we have precious little biographical data. Catholics seem to take the Annunciation in the Gospel of Luke 1:26–56 as their starting point in understanding Mary, which includes the great Marian prayer called the Magnificat (Luke 1:46–55). The Gospel of Luke records the angel Gabriel's visit to the young Mary, who was a virgin betrothed to a man named Joseph, in the town of Nazareth in Galilee. The angel's message to Mary was disturbing.

> "Do not be afraid, Mary, for you have found favor with God. And now you will conceive in your womb and bear a son, and you will name him Jesus." Mary replied, "How can this be, since I am a virgin?" "Nothing will be impossible with God." Then Mary said, "Here I am, let it be with me according to your word." (Luke 1:29–31, 34, 37–38 NRSV).

Through the story of Mary we see what our own life of love in God is capable of becoming.[4] While we cannot know, of course, with certainty what Mary thought and felt, we can legitimately speculate, with a certain confidence, regarding her way of life, values, and style of relating to God and others, including her son, Jesus. Mary's receptivity to inner possibilities, her capacity to ponder and reflect, and her engagement in dialogue with God offer us insights into what is possible for us. In a mystical experience, St. Alphonse Liguori is said to have heard Mary say at the Annunciation, "What use, Gabriel, is this message if it is given only to me and not everyone else?"

Her Uniqueness

We turn our attention to some of the unique features in Mary's personality that invite us to consider the model of faith she is. Mary is portrayed as a person capable of *pondering* in depth. As a matter of fact, she gives new substance to the meaning of the word. Scripture testifies to this characteristic in Mary. Hearing the unsettling information told by the shepherds to Mary and Joseph at the birth of Jesus, the Gospel records: "As for Mary, she treasured all these things and pondered them in her heart" (Luke 2:19 NJB). When faced with losing the twelve-year-old Jesus, frantically searching for him for three days and finding him in the Temple without remorse for the worry he caused his parents, the Gospel simply states: "His mother stored up all these things in her heart" (Luke 2:51).

Later, when Mary goes looking for Jesus, she finds him in the midst of a crowd and is unable to reach him. Someone tells Jesus his mother is "standing outside and wants to see you" (Luke 8:19–20). The Gospel records that Jesus apparently dismisses her request and tells the crowd that "my mother and my brothers are those who hear the word of God and put it into practice" (Luke 8:21). On one level it looks as though Jesus failed to respond to the presence of his mother; the deeper look reveals Jesus suggesting his own mother as a model disciple, one who hears the word of God and lives from the divine mandate. We are left to imagine the crowd turning to Mary to catch a glimpse of her response, to see if she felt a rebuke or, unable to see or touch him, whether she understood yet again and once more the implications of her pondering and holding these things in her heart (Luke 8:19–21; Mark 3:31–35; Matthew 12:46–50).

Her pondering spirit must have existed prior to the angelic invitation. Her ability to hold things in her heart suggests to us that Mary's inner life made her susceptible to the inner hearing of God's voice. Here we see in Mary a feature of the *inhearing* and spiritual *conversio* (meaning "transformative dialogue") characteristic of those who are friends of God. Mary was familiar with the story of Moses in the Torah and the biblical prophets of old. Mary flows in that same stream of those who hear and talk with God. "Such a life of love in God necessarily involves communing with God, or 'dialogical' experience. All love demands communing in ever-greater intensity. Mary's continuing dialogue with God is the primary expression of her inner freedom" (Jegen 1985, pp. 152, 158). It is clear from the few other references in Scripture that Mary related to others, including her son, with an authenticity of expression, unafraid to speak her mind, ask her questions, and ponder what she heard.

Thus, it is not surprising that in 1854 when the dogma of the Immaculate Conception was proclaimed, Mary is so named as "always conversant with God."

One cannot help but speculate further on her personality as one unsullied by a suffocating ego and passions out of control. Surely, she was well schooled in a life of inner discipline and outwardly in charge of herself. Mary was/is the underground cable, the conduit through which salvation – liberation and wholeness – came/comes to us.

Jesus was the Trumpeter of the Good News; Mary was the birth canal through which the Trumpeter's salvific music could be heard. The feminine and masculine joined in their own particular way so that the work of salvation could be achieved. Jesus, the Trumpeter, and Mary, the Reed, sang together the Hymn of Salvation revealing that the feminine and masculine cooperate, relate, play, suffer, and sing the symphony of praise that was God's intention in creation. What mutual strength! What shared power! What love made manifest!

> *You went away
> but never left us.*
>
> —St. John Chrysostom in
> a colloquy with Mary

Mary in the Life Cycle

Mary is a surprising model for teenagers, which is the developmental or life-cycle stage, biblically speaking, at which we first meet her. Jewish teenagers of that day would not have had the sexual hang-ups handed down to us by Puritanism and Jansenism. Thoughts of her future vocation as wife, mother, maker of the sanctuary of the Jewish home and table would have been prominent. Teen years are usually the ones during which thoughts about our life interests and work is best considered. In our twenty-first-century culture, at least in the United States, enormous amounts of time and money are spent on misdirecting adolescents toward consumerism of fleeting, one-dimensional glitz and sensationalism. Teenagers are killed for their jackets, sneakers, and jewelry; one must be part of the faceless crowd. Unfortunately, this does not end with the teen years. Too many, uncritically absorbed by the lures of the culture, enter adulthood taking on a false sense of self and end up copycats or imitators instead of originals.

Originality begins in the womb. We are meant to be cultivated to a blooming state. Mary was and is an original who intensified the lines and colors of her personhood by development of a healthy psyche, intellect, memory, and spirit. This was manifested at the time of the meeting with Gabriel. She was surprised by the visit, and more so by the message. Her common sense remained intact as she responded to the surprise by asking essential questions. Going out on a limb was not her idea of a good move. Her integrity as a woman was at stake. How could she be a single mother? Joseph was only a fiancé, not a husband. Mary's main interest was not in being a star but in being a person of honor. She lost no time in seeking counsel to cope with the message she had embraced as truth. In fact, she was so unself-conscious as to set out on foot to visit her older cousin, Elizabeth.

We have in Mary the realization that a teen can indeed manage her life quite well. She possessed the capacity to hear the prodding of the Spirit, the willingness to be overshadowed by its power, to carry to fruition the life within her, to face into fear, take the risk of the mysterious carrying out of God's promise to Israel. In Mary we see that self-interest and individualism are not the values and virtues of the God-bearers we are all called to be.

If we don't believe in Divine Presence and Power, we become derelicts in the hands of self-centeredness, complacency, and superficiality. We have to develop a strong psyche, a disciplined, single-minded intellect and a deep spirituality as did Mary. Pondering and treasuring in her heart were second nature to her. The teenage Mary, the widowed mature Mary, the middle-aged Mary at the foot of the cross, each models the kind of receptivity to God's grace that is our destiny. It is congruent with God's nature to share divine life with God's creatures created in God's own image and likeness, male and female alike. Such grace is at our disposal but only in so far as we are open to receive and engage this Presence and Power. There is no coercion or manipulation in the Divine nature. Had Mary not said "yes" to God's favor, it would not have been possible for God to be made human in Jesus, son of Mary, the woman of Nazareth. One wonders if other women were asked and declined until Mary? Mary is an original, and in her we see the feminine face of God.

> *What good is it to me*
> *if Mary is full of grace*
> *if I am not full of grace too?*
> —Meister Eckhart

Ordinary is the word that could be used to describe her outer life. Joseph was an artisan who had to satisfy his customers. Mary kept house, cared for her husband, and trained her son in the culture, customs, and mores of the time. She was the first to teach him prayer, tell him the stories of the faith of ancient Israel, and show him how to set the table of hospitality and hope. They lived in Nazareth, which was about as good a place as Podunk. Jesus neither went to the synagogue, nor to any Ivy League prep school, nor was Gamaliel his tutor. Public education was his in the shade of the Holy Spirit. Of course, as already said, much of this is speculation since we have no inkling as to all that shaped the interior motives and drives of Jesus or Mary. The gospels are about proclamation of good news and not biography. We use our intelligence and imagination to enter Mary's story and make it our own.

One of the lessons of Mary's outer ordinary life is that each of us has, as did Mary, Jesus, and Joseph, a work to claim and complete. And a work is not synonymous with a job. Mary had a job, if you will, as a wife, mother, daughter, and neighbor, but her WORK was to be an instrument of redemption, a woman of love, a servant of God's vision.

This lovely woman grew in grace and wisdom. She raised her son, watched him grow as an artisan like his father, and must have wished for him to stay near after she buried Joseph and was left alone. She lived in the dark of mystery. She waited in prayerful patience. What an artist of life!

Mary was a woman of sensitivity and awareness. The dark signs of her son's mission to move on must have begun to pierce her heart, as Simeon prophesied (Luke 2:35). By twelve, he made it clear that Yahweh's work was primary. Came the day which all mothers dread, an empty house. Her son loved the will of Abba "more than these." She released him from her hearth to the world, to the wolves, with a mother's love, which is all over again the birth pangs of letting a child be born again into his or her very own life. She could not have known but she was sending forth the Sacrificial Lamb!

Her son became known. People talked. Within their familial circle, there was discomfort with Jesus' preaching and teaching. The Gospel of Mark records:

> He went home again, and once more such a crowd collected that they could not even have a meal. When his relations heard of this, they set out to take charge of him; they said, "He is out of his mind." (Mark 3:20–21 NJB)

She, who sought not fame, was his mother. She listened with concern and anxiety and loving surprise at the grandeur of this man, her son. Her kinfolk thought Jesus deranged (a judgment that must have cut deep), yet her women friends encircled her with belief and service. Mary had an early faith community of women. What sharing must have been theirs! Jewish wives, mothers, and prostitutes revealed a special kind of strong, loyal intimacy.

Tradition refers to the record of Jesus' brief active ministry as his public life. The gospels tell the story of his hunger to walk the way and ways of truth and justice. He is met with resistance and mocking. The stench of the evil must have bombarded Mary as it enveloped her son. What loneliness must have overpowered each of them at different times? Yet the momentum of his message and mission could not be stopped. Mary watched, listened, pondered, and prayed. These years were a mixture of joy and sadness: joy that her son was clear and steady about his work, and sad that so much of his effort seemed futile.

By her faithful commitment, Mary lived the truth that nothing is lost by holding fast to integrity. And the very worst was still to come. Mary must have seen it coming, just as we often intuit some imminent catastrophe. While the scriptural evidence is slim, it seems clear that Mary neither denied the gravity of the situation nor ran away from it. She saw the dilemma as it was: the conflict of good and evil, though she may not have named it so. Her pondering so many things in her heart may have given her the wisdom to know that fear of the unknown and hardness of heart would not prevail because deep in her stored memory there was the angel's voice, "nothing is impossible with God" (Luke 1:37). Maybe her own Magnificat filled her inner senses with the assurance that God does not forget those upon whom God's favor rests (Luke 1:46–55).

The woman, acquainted with the mystery of sorrow, was certainly aware that Jesus' decision to go to Jerusalem was ominous and necessary. We know she was with Jesus on Calvary. The Gospel of John in understated elegance notes: "Near the cross of Jesus stood his mother" and the small band of women friends (John 19:25 NJB). Mary listens to a final word from son to mother giving her over to the care of another. "'Woman,' (pointing to his beloved John), 'this is your son.' Then to the disciple he said, 'This is your mother.' And from that hour the disciple took her into his home" (John 19:26–27). In the end, she bears the double cross of losing her son and being put in the care of another, losing her own home. Her understanding of the plight of the elderly of our age would be profound. Mary, among women, bore an acute understanding of what mothers and fathers experience who lose their children to noble or ignoble causes. Her son, Jesus, in the prime of life, struggled in a world that failed to understand him and then "they" took him from her. Being left behind as the sad mother of a criminal was heavy indeed, but more than that heaviness was the felt loss of his presence.

His apostles, disciples, and the women who followed Jesus became a family, her family. She knew her son in ways that they did not. The gospel story is just a patchwork of fragments but one is led to ponder that the warmth of her understanding must have been a healing balm for guilty, grief-stricken followers. In the fear-laden upper room, Mary, now the mother of the crucified Jesus, stayed with those who had failed and even denied her son when he needed them most. No wonder Mary is named "Mother of Good Counsel" and "Comforter of the Afflicted." She, who yearned for the sight and living embrace of her son, as all mothers do, found that place in her pondering heart for a heroic forgiveness and a compassion without condition. Only one verse in the Acts of the Apostles provides this testimony; yet this one verse says volumes:

> With one heart all these joined constantly in prayer, together with some women, including Mary the mother of Jesus, and with his brothers. (Acts 1:14 NJB)

Mary stayed the course of life and love's challenges. Patient trust born of deep faith was her trademark to the end. She completed the work committed to her care.

The Dark Night of the Morning Star

Finally, an important aspect of Mary's life and her son's was their experience of darkness and the absence of God. No one can escape the dark side of life. Mary "most venerable" is also Mary "most vulnerable." Hearing the Voice, feeling the Presence, and seeing the messenger is only part of the mystery of life with God. The experience of the dark opposite will follow just as night follows day. How do we speak of this dark night and give it the same value as the morning star? Darkness is the atmosphere conducive to rest and sleep, but it is also an experience of abandonment and profound desolation. Once the conversation with the angel ended, Mary must have worked at a deep interior level to discern how to live out the implications of her "yes." As did Jesus, she must have had bouts with inner darkness. She knew the ache of loneliness, the fear of rejection, the future's uncertainty. She knew this for herself and felt it empathically with her child. No wonder she is called "Seat of Wisdom," "Strength of the Broken-hearted," "Sign of

Contradiction," and "Spiritual Vessel," as well as many other pertinent symbols of availability.[5]

At times darkness results from too much light. The light has to filter through our density until we accept it and put it to good use in everyday living. To make light is to make shadow; they exist in tandem. While we don't know explicitly about Mary's interior darkness, we can imagine her Gethsemane and Golgotha. In Mary, we see who we can become. No wonder she is called "Cause of our Joy."

> *Mary, Dark Night of the Morning Star, guide us.*

A Colloquy on Being a Woman or a Man

The biological and existential fact that we are either a man or a woman would appear to be brazenly obvious. Yet our experience of being male or female and our attempts to develop intimacy as friends or soulmates is wrought with ambiguities. Progoff's work includes considerations about the *event* of being a woman or a man. He presents us with a self-reflective process that helps us establish an inner relationship with our experience of being a man with the interplay of masculinity and femininity within or being a woman with the interplay of femininity and masculinity within. As with our previous experience of Ignatian colloquy, in this exercise we attempt to become aware of our femaleness or maleness. We try to let the reality of our manliness or womanliness have voice and speak to us with openness and fluidity (Progoff 1992, pp. 167–181).

Quiet yourself by first reciting aloud and then silently one of the following litanies:

> *Woman of divine grace, speak within me.*
> *Woman of good counsel, speak within me.*
> *Woman most powerful, speak within me.*
> *Woman most compassionate, speak within me.*
> *Mirror of justice, illumine me.*
> *Seat of wisdom, illumine me.*

Spiritual vessel, guide me.
Vessel of honor, guide me.
Mystical rose, open me.
Tower of ivory, strengthen me.
House of gold, strengthen me.
Ark of the covenant, sustain me.
Morning star, awaken me.

When you are sufficiently focused, begin writing in free-flowing style how you experienced being a little girl or little boy. Identify and describe five key stories about being you as a little boy or girl that took place within the first ten years of your life. There is a story within the event of your being born a girl or a boy; allow yourself to recover five key memories of that story now. This writing is meant to heighten your awareness of the gift and/or burden of being female or male, be it pleasant, painful, rich, or paltry; *it is yours*.

When you are finished, rest briefly and proceed by following the same pattern of reflection for your adolescence. For this period of your life, identify the five stories that capture for you your experience of being of girl becoming a woman or a boy becoming a man. Focus on the years from age thirteen to twenty-two. Do not censure or control what arises as a story. Simply record it as it unfolds within your memory.

When you are finished, rest briefly and follow the same pattern of reflection for your young adulthood, adulthood, middle age, older age, and beyond, depending on how much of the life cycle forms the repertoire of your lived experience!

Reread what you have written. Today, what would you say are the most significant influences and circumstances that shaped your sense of being a female or a male self?

So much goes into shaping our primary identity. As we grow in freedom and grace, we make choices that alter, refashion, and reshape our selves in light of our growth beyond self-limiting conceptions of our personhood received through parents, family, historical influences, culture, religion, etc. In our adulthood, we consciously re-embrace and claim for ourselves those positive reinforcements we received as little children from parents, family, history, culture, and religion. The decisions we make about how we will live our womanhood or manhood adjust our childhood experiences and can shift limiting warrants and negative reinforce-ments experienced at other times in our development. It is never to late to become the woman or man that is our radiant self, a self designed and destined to reflect God's own image.

It is now time for a colloquy with the woman or the man that is you. Greet her or him and let the conversation begin. Speak from your depth to the depth of the woman or man who wishes to speak in you and to you. Allow the exchange to flow in unfettered, undirected dialogue. Record it as it comes without editing. He or she will speak through your pen. When the dialogue is finished, remain for a moment in silence.

Reread the dialogue and note in your journal how it feels to have had this conversation and any other insights or responses that seem important for you to record. Date your entry.

> *You are a very wise old woman*
> *and a very wise old man.*
>
> —Ira Progoff to Irene Dugan, r.c.

Notes

1. In 1996, William J. O'Malley, SJ, published a second edition of a book enti-tled *The Fifth Week.* O'Malley speaks of the themes of the four weeks of the Ignatian Exercises and says that the fifth week is the rest of one's life. Irene Dugan may have been familiar with this book and chose to give a more specif-ic focus to the fifth week by naming it "The Woman." *Ed.*

2. *Theotokos* is the title bestowed upon Mary at the Council of Ephesus in 431 C.E.

3. For a more detailed explanation of the image of God in human sexuality as represented in Genesis 2–3, see Phyllis Trible, *God and the Rhetoric of Sexuality* (1978).

4. The following sources assisted in clarifying Sister Dugan's thoughts: Carol Frances Jegen, B.V.M., "Mary Immaculate: Woman of Freedom, Patroness of the United States" (Jegen 1985, pp. 143–161) and "Mary and the Future of the Church" (Eigo 1994, pp. 175–202); and Karl Rahner, *Mary, Mother of the Lord* (1963).

5. See Richo (2001) for historical information on the development of the Litany of Loreto (1200 C.E.).

10. Epilogue

❦

Editor's Introduction

The Spiritual Exercises of St. Ignatius, structured on a thirty-day or four-week model, officially conclude with the contemplation on God's love. Sister Dugan chose to reflect on the meaning and mystery of divine love through the lens of transformational spirituality. In chapter 7, she correlated Ignatius's Contemplatio Ad Amorem *with insights from Progoff on the importance of being intentional about a life vision.*

Interestingly, Ignatius included substantial additional material in a final section added to the Exercises. These Ignatian "rules" or guidelines provide additional insights and methods for the serious spiritual seeker (see Fleming 1996, pp. 183–291). Ignatius included the following as supplementary material:

Three Methods of Praying

The Mysteries of the Life of Christ

Rules for Perceiving and Knowing in Some Manner the Different Movements That Are Caused in the Soul or Guidelines for the Discernment of Spirits

The Meaning of Spiritual Consolation and Desolation

The Ministry of Distribution of Alms or Guidelines to the Sharing of Wealth and Possessions

Notes Concerning Scruples

To Have the True Sentiment Which We Ought in the Church Militant or Guidelines for Thinking with the Church Today

Sister Dugan chose to conclude her reflections on the natural or process spirituality of Ignatius of Loyola, integrated with a variety of Progoff's insights, with a final chapter entitled "Epilogue." Her epilogue takes on the character of one of the definitions of the meaning of the word: a speech delivered by one of the actors at the end of a play. This chapter especially conveys Sister Dugan's particular flare for the dramatic. She seems to be giving a final speech of sorts, offering us insights into the testament of the priorities of her own spiritual vision.

Differing from Ignatius's ordering of his supplement to the Spiritual Exercises, Sister Dugan begins her final chapter with a reference back to Ignatius's Third Week rules, the guidelines for eating. I believe this is a literary guise for her to make a statement on the lost art of eating and drinking with conscious relish, something she loved and expected of those dining in her company. She also returns to the theme of the importance of relationship with one's own body, a thread in Progoff's work as well. One senses her self-awareness of the limitations imposed by her own confinement in a wheelchair and the power of her cultivated memory to stimulate our own self-awareness, as she makes autobiographical references to memories of her youth romping in the ocean waves of the Jersey shore.

Precisely because this chapter is Irene's written epilogue, as well as her conclusion to this labor of love, I present it here with minimal editing.

IGNATIUS WAS A MAN OF PRAYER WHO DID ALL IN HIS POWER TO help others to experience the power of praying. Ignatius thought of every angle and avenue of our lives that calls for attention and awareness in decision-making through growth in self-knowledge. He set up what he calls "rules" at the end of the Exercises, which today is more broadly named "guidelines" by Fleming, but might also be called considerations or, my preference, stargazing.

Considerations About Eating

We live in an era of no leisure. In fact, we seem not to know what is meant by *leisure* and its necessity in our daily life. We rush, rush, rush, even when there is nothing to which we are rushing.

The rush is particularly noticeable in our eating habits. Fast food is our daily body preoccupation. Eating/drinking as we walk the streets, ride in buses or cars seems to be a way of life. The final act of horror is dropping the containers of our food just any place but never in a disposal can or basket.

This suggests a grossness, which makes us people of no manners or thoughtfulness. Drinking out of bottles and cans is common-place practice, even out of milk cartons and juice bottles. Such behavior doesn't speak well about how we think about ourselves. It is the "in thing" to be sloppy and careless!

If so, that may account in part for our attitude about the Holy Eucharist, a meal commemorating the giving of himself by Jesus to save us from ourselves and retrieve for us our lost inheritance, Heaven. How easy it seems for us to fall into rote mindlessness about our partaking of the bread of life and the cup that binds us together in faith.

Jesus is part of the tradition of hospitality that welcomes a guest with graciousness and warmth. He is a man who knows the mores of the moment at table. Breaking bread with someone means we have a felt experience of or desire for solidarity with that one.

We eat, drink, sleep, work, and play in order to insure good health for our bodies *and* for our whole being. Ergo, the way we *nourish* ourselves commands attention and loving care. Our whole being requires attention regarding what we take in and what we give out. I am not speaking here of the false religiosity that includes Lenten fasting to lose weight or the cultural preoccupation of modern times with the slim-thin affair whose goal is to make us more "attractive."

Ignatius presents us with a mindful approach about the ordinary daily activity of eating. He suggests as we eat, preferably at table, that we reflect on the table-fellowship of Jesus and his friends and the beautiful, almost lost, art of Hebrew ancestry of the sacrality of eating together. People gloss over a genuine prayer of thanks before eating. People hardly take time to eat. To think that people would take the leisure of conversing together about the joy of eating, think together aloud about the deeper meaning of sharing the table or the realms of nourishment we receive from each other seems ridiculous today. Many families almost pride themselves on talking about how rarely they eat together, which may indeed be a bravado that disguises their hunger for such times of shared intimacy in the sanctuary of their own home. Such realms of conversation seem relegated to exceptional settings, such as retreats.

Centuries ago, Ignatius thought it important to leave "rules" for the most human action of eating. His focus on conscious attending to what and how we eat clearly foreshadowed the late-twentieth-century mind-body-spirit interests. While certainly not completely free of the dualism syndrome in Christianity, Ignatius evidences again and again a basic trust in the physical and affective dimensions of being human. For Ignatius, eating is an aspect of the training ground for the spiritual discipline of moderation in all things and living with an awareness of the connections between our physical self and the development of an inner life. Progoff shares these same considerations. Progoff sharpens our insights into the truth that our physical life is larger than our own particular body since it is through our bodies that "we seek to deepen our relationship with the physical world in all its aspects" (1992, p. 154). We need to take more opportunities to experience how essential, how revelatory-sacramental are these bones and flesh of ours, which each day literally carry us into and through life.

Colloquy with the Body

It seems fitting, at this juncture, to explore a body-spirit connection. Progoff explains this method in detail in *At a Journal Workshop* (1992, pp. 154–166). Our body knows more about us than anyone, other than God, and very often more than we allow ourselves to know. Our bodiliness is the most obvious mark of our very existence. We experience life through our body.

> Our bodies have a natural wisdom with a warming system, a healing system, and a recuperating system. Our experiences of exaltation as well as of pain come to us through our body and that is one main reason why we are accustomed to think of our bodies as supremely private. Our body is the instrument for our most inti-

mate relationships and our most meaningful participation in the life process as a whole. The life of our body parallels the movement of our personal life. (Progoff 1992, p. 155)

Our body is the storage place of our memories. Even our muscles carry memories. Our cells have memories. It is not uncommon in the act of receiving a massage that the masseur or masseuse, in rubbing or kneading various parts of our bodies, evokes feelings in us, stirs memories, producing tears. If we wish to establish a relationship with our body, we must explore its life history. The body has a story of its own to tell. As Progoff says, "The body of a human being functions by principles that are universal in the species, but each individual body is unique. Each begins with a different seed-nature unfolding in its own time in its own particular environment. Each body builds through the years its own life history with its unique combination of growth and illness and activity" (Progoff 1992, p. 155).

Please enter a period of Sabbath rest in order to move with ease from outer preoccupations to the stillness within. Repeat aloud and then silently this verse from the Book of Numbers:

"God of the spirits of all flesh," enter into my midst.
(Numbers 27:16 NRSV)

Have your journal at hand.
Sit now in quietness and turn your mindful and soulful attention to recollecting memories of your physical life. As a start, you may say out loud phrases that come to you, such as,

"I recall running to greet my father. "
"Having the measles."
"Playing basketball."
"Summers at the Jersey shore."
"Dancing."
"Never walking again."

The phrases may be many or few. You are allowing the deep story of your physical self to emerge so that you can receive information about your life through the story of your own body.

Note in your journal the emotional responses that stir from retrieving these memories and let yourself feel the continuity of movement in your body's history.

The rereading gives a sense of your relationship with your body and how you feel about your body in the now. Remain in quiet to compose a focusing statement about this relationship with your body. What is the situation between you and your body? Write a brief, *nonjudgmental* statement describing your attitudes and actions towards your physical self. Let it be an honest reflection on how you feel about your body. Let the words emerge that most authentically reflect what it is you need to say about this most intimate relationship.

In stillness, *feel into* the life of your body. Allow any images, sensations, or awarenesses to pass before you without holding onto or trying to repress them. Simply behold what goes on. You are now ready to have a colloquy with your body.

Let yourself feel the inner continuity of the life of the body. Speak to it. Greet it. Say whatever comes to you. Record what you say. Let the give and take of the colloquy have the natural rhythm of a conversation.

When the procession of exchange comes to a halt, remain in quiet silence. Be attentive to any unfinished business that still seeks expression in the colloquy or acknowledge that the exchange has ended and let it rest for now. It is helpful to reread all you have written, being aware of any feelings and insights that arise. Add these at the close of the exercise. Date your entry.

This colloquy with your body helps you appreciate your physical life as a great gift from God. You will exercise, rest, play, eat, dance and express yourself through it with joy, care, and love. You will want to do more dialogues with your body as you deepen your inner life as a whole. The body is the temple of the soul, the meeting ground of all experience. It does us well to relish a visceral theology that treasures the carnality of grace and the grace of carnality (cf. Keen 1970, p. 47).

Three Methods of Praying

In the conclusion of the Spiritual Exercises, St. Ignatius proposes three ways of praying: meditation, contemplation, and application of the senses. Just to be sure we do not give up on dry days, he adds three approaches for mindful prayer and reflection (Fleming 1996, pp. 185–198). These are meant to be preparatory means to deepen the experience of prayer, yet preparing for prayer is, in a sense, praying itself.

The first way suggests we reflect on the Ten Words (Ex. 20:11–17), on major compulsions, on our intellect, will, imagination and memory, and the great gift of our fine external and internal senses.

This is not a Pollyanna approach or one of avoidance. In fact, it is a great and narrow road to travel toward *self-knowledge*. Take for example the Ten Words (commonly called the Ten Commandments). One can gloss over them with a shrug, saying "shall nots" are not for me.

Let's have a go at it.

First Word: Thou shalt not have strange gods before me.

Of course, you never have strange gods before the real God! Really? How about money, power over others, lots of possessions, or a great hankering for more of everything? Just how many people or things come before God? If nothing hit you hard here, you may be either a saint or a great liar and evader.

Second Word: Thou shalt not take the name of the Lord, your God, in vain.

Listen to the ordinary jargon of our day and your own. The Lord's name is used as an expletive, as a by-the-way expression. Nothing is sacred about this Holy Name. The Jews held it so sacred they would not even utter the name.

Third Word: Remember – keep holy the Sabbath.

The Sabbath! Whoever heard of that except as a day to do all I couldn't do during the week! Play golf or tennis, do the work, paint the house. God? Oh! He's around, I guess.

Fourth Word: Honor the father and mother.

This does not mean we approve of how they raised us or their lifestyle but that we must thank them for giving us life, the most sacred God-given gift that has placed us on the world stage. We accept them as they are and not as we wish they were. This acceptance includes where *they* came from, how *they* were raised and the beliefs imposed on each of them. Dumping them as used articles is not honoring them. Freeing ourselves from their clinging *is* to honor them.

Fifth Word: Thou shalt not kill.

Killing is a terrible action against life. Think of all the government legislation pro and con against the preservation of life . . . polluted waters, air, earth, livestock, fruits and vegetables that sustain life. Then the big issue of guns. All of this boils down to the fact that LIFE is no longer held SACRED. Part of it is due to the prevalent atmosphere of HATE. Hate is a killer widespread in its venom. Reflect on the question: "Whom would *I* like to kill?" and you will find you end up with a shockingly long list. The act of killing transcends the physical; there are so many ways to kill the spirit.

Sixth Word: Thou shalt not commit adultery.

This is the dishonoring of a man's or woman's most intimate companion. Films and advertisements flaunt their advocacy of such an act.

Seventh Word: Thou shalt not steal.

This word speaks to our tendencies to the self-indulgent taking of possessions, including ideas that do not belong to us. Pickpockets and shoplifters galore who cause prices to skyrocket in order to compensate for this behavior. Commodities that folks need, such as their credit cards, cars, phone, and radios, simply stolen away. And the more horrendous state of our teenage population – stealing and killing for leather jackets, gym shoes, backpacks, and any item they feel they are somehow entitled to take. How about all the devious efforts we make to steal away a most treasured right: a person's good name. Do we actually think that gossip, backbiting, and slander are not on the slippery slope of violating the seventh and eighth words?

Eighth Word: Thou shalt not bear false witness against your neighbor.

While going about the workday for which we are being paid, how much time do we devote to gossip, blaming, and dumping our own responsibilities on another? "I didn't do it, someone else did." This is an everyday occurrence we hardly notice. Think of the number of people actually in jail because of trumped up and framed situations. We are all part of this dilemma.

Ninth Word: Thou shalt not covet your neighbor's house, or your neighbor's spouse.

We live these days in such fear and self-protection precisely because we feel that the safety and sacrality of our home and hearth is easily assaulted. The bonds of trust in committed relationships have far too often grown threadbare and breed the condition for infidelities, of which we sadly enjoy the gossipy insinuations and jokes.

Tenth Word: Thou shalt not covet your neighbor's goods.

The archaic word *covet* keeps appearing. It means a misdirected desire; to wish a wrongful desire without due regard for the rights and needs of others. We cannot avoid exploring the force of deep envy in our lives. "It isn't fair" for someone to have more than I. "I have just as much right to . . . ." Such attitudes build rancor and even revenge in our hearts. We want *more* than we need or will ever use.

Vices and Virtues

Following this examination of consciousness, which relies on the wisdom of the Word, Ignatius proceeds to invite the journeyer in faith to muster the courage to explore the "seven deadly sins": pride, anger, envy, lust, gluttony, avarice, and sloth (Fleming 1996, pp. 187–189). Fleming says, "In contrast with the commandments which are to be faithfully observed, we are now reflecting upon sins or patterns of behavior to be avoided" (ibid., p. 189). Just the saying of the words makes you want to run away. We may at first glance think we are riddled with all seven!

Actually, holistic depth psychology has given us a new lens from which to view these potentially destructive forces in our lives. Sixteenth-century Ignatius talks about the operation of these vices as "compulsions," actually quite unavoidable in the human condition. Modern insights prompted by the personality and sacred science of holistic depth psychology has produced an invention called the Enneagram. The term *Enneagram* derives from the Greek word *ennea,* meaning "nine," and *gram,* meaning "a figure or something drawn." The Enneagram is represented as a diagram or star with nine points representing nine personality patterns. The Enneagram is a theory of personality types that describes nine distinct and fundamentally different patterns of thinking, feeling, and acting. The nine types are (1) the perfectionist, (2) the giver, (3) the performer, (4) the romantic, (5) the observer, (6) the loyal skeptic, (7) the epicure, (8) the protector, and (9) the mediator. According to David Daniels and Helen Palmer (2003), "As you discover your personality type and the underlying basic proposition, you will also discover what motivates you, your coping strategy, and keys to personal development." The nine types teach us that each one of the so-called deadly sins is a compulsion that lurks within the individual personality. Our task is not to deny our capacities for pride, anger, envy, lust, excess, greed, and apathy; but to own them and work to mitigate their destructiveness in our lives. The Enneagram is just one more way of widening consciousness; it is a healthy avenue for our natural striving toward wholeness and holiness. The study and practice of the Enneagram is extremely freeing and enlightening. One discovers that the humble ownership of a compulsion is a path to enlightenment. This kind of humility does not mean biting the dust but discovering my place in the great economy of creation.

The Powers of the Soul

I call this a very important "stargazing" time of prayer. As we learn to relish the simple gift of eating well, so we are invited not to lose sight of those precious intangible gifts of the faculties of the spirit: intellect, will, memory, and, I must add, imagination (Fleming 1996, p. 189). Take some time to consider how you use your mind, your ability to think, to figure out simple and complex matters. I've heard it said that we use only a fraction of our brain's capacity. Consider how fortunate you are to have such a gift to plan your life, think about decisions, and enter into discernment about them.

The intellect when joined to the electric pulse of the imagination opens up our creative genius to push the will to performance. We begin to imitate God.

Memory stores all the experience of our life. Our memories, which by nature of being a memory are about the past, also hold lessons for the present and future. Reliance on memory can teach us the pluses and minuses about that which will promote growth and what deters it. Thus, we can become wise and full of grace (divine energy), as well as a model for others.

Developing and trusting these powers of psyche and soul moves us in the direction of wise decision-making, decisions that are part of the process of *choosing life.*

On the Five Senses of the Body

Ignatius provides us with another avenue for self-knowledge, which is a consideration of and reflection on our five senses. Awakening our senses of seeing, hearing, smelling, tasting, and touching has been explored in previous chapters. It is interesting that Ignatius refers to the senses yet again to underscore that continued inner growth requires continued development of our outer senses. They are our bridge into the world we negotiate each day.

A good way to investigate your relationship with your five senses is to return to the method of a colloquy. My preference is to do this meditation in the summer season and actually take myself into nature's beauty to fill up the senses. You could, however, enter this dialogue through the exercise of your memory and imagination. You can see why these powers of the soul expand your spiritual repertoire.

> On a nice sunny day, find a quiet place to be alone by a river, a lake, a park, or a forest preserve. Quiet yourself interiorly to concentrate on your senses. Have your journal available, but write nothing until you have listened to each sense.
>
> Begin by asking your eyes, "What have I made you look at very often?" Then *listen* for a reply. Don't allow arguments or defenses to move in.

Then ask your ears, "What do I let you listen to every day?" Again, listen to the response.

Ask your nose, "What kind of pollution have I let you breathe day after day?" Also, "What kind of smells are you exposed to regularly?" Then again, just listen.

Say to your mouth, "What is the color of the words I have you speak, and what have I put into you that is detrimental to my whole being?" Again, LISTEN.

Your hands are made for caressing, healing and creating. Say to them, "How have I used you to create a good environment, help a hurting one, reach out in love in any kind of situation?" Or, "How have I slapped another, pushed someone around and shown no respect?" How do I touch? Again, LISTEN.

While retaining the sense of being aware of your senses, repeat the questions slowly, this time making a response to what you hear each sense saying to you. Record the dialogue in your journal. Date your entry.

As I said earlier in this epilogue, you will want to do more collo-quies with your body as you deepen your inner life as a whole. Each of our outer senses is matched with a similar inner sense and when freed to grow together enhance our sense of being alive, of spiritual enlargement.

The Second Way

The second method of prayer proposed by Ignatius encourages the activation of the senses to taste and savor each word of a prayer, such as the "Our Father" (Fleming 1996, pp. 191–197).

We begin by focusing our gaze inward, recalling the words of the "Our Father." You may sit, kneel, or stand as your body indicates as appropriate. You may choose to substitute the Aramaic word *Abba* for "Father," since this is the word Jesus used and it carries a sense of the intimacy of calling our God "mommy" or "daddy," thus enabling us to be a child of God, no matter how old we are. Roll one word at a time around your mouth and heart, allowing the taste of the word to alert you to its beauty and meaning. Stay at each word as long as you are consoled. If an hour passes and you have tasted only a few words, offer a prayer of praise and thanks to God with the intention of finishing the whole prayer at another time. This is a refreshing and quieting experience.

This method suggested by Ignatius is quite similar to what I described earlier as a mantra. Progoff says, "While there are a number of other terms to describe the meditative process of making deeper contact, they tend to refer to practices that depend on doctrines within their own framework of belief. Because of the pluralistic nature of religious experience, especially at this point in history, it seemed to me to be essential to have a term that would not be identified with any particular doctrine" (1992, pp. 328–329). Therefore, Progoff, whose aims are similar to Ignatius, opens the horizon by utilizing the mantra. A mantra refers to anything that serves as an aid to the quieting of the self. It is a means to the climate of inner stillness that creates the condition for the inner senses to be awakened.

Progoff recommends that we touch into our own life to draw forth seven-syllable phrases that express something deep and personal. The basis of this is the ancient Eastern art of breathing. Most modern people breathe superficially and in a state of unawareness of the importance of breathing. Genesis records that God breathed into 'adam [the earth creature] the breath of life (Genesis 2:7). Breathing is essential to life *and* a discipline of serenity.

Experiment now with the simple breathing exercise by following the steps suggested by Thich Nhat Hanh (a Vietnamese Buddhist monk and author of *The Miracle of Mindfulness: A Manual on Meditation*). Sit in a relaxed position (lotus position if you wish). Notice your breathing. Softly say, "in" as you breath in and "out" as you expel air. Do this as long as necessary for your breathing to become rhythmic. Next, move to softly saying, "deep" as you breath in and "slow" as you breath out. The next words are "calm" and "ease," and the last two are "smile" and "release." This exercise centers you in the present. It is a wonderful moment.

Quiet centeredness and calm will flow in, around, and over you through the gentle discipline of centered breathing.

The Ministry of Almsgiving

In the final pages of the Spiritual Exercises, Ignatius includes guidelines directed at a specific group of Christians committed to works of justice and charity. His guidelines are directed toward those almsgivers who go about providing for the needs of the poor. These considerations about the sharing of one's wealth and possessions seem particularly apt at the close of the Ignatian spiritual experience (Fleming 1992, pp. 269–273). Pilgrims on the spiritual journey clearly see that there is a social dimension to taking one's inner life seriously. Personal spirituality spills over into lifestyle. Sharing is a great part of life: notice how, in times of disaster, people reach out to each other in surprisingly selfless kinds of ways.

Besides considering sharing one's wealth and possessions, there is the matter of developing and sharing one's talents and aptitudes. I am referring here to the balance between the outer and the inner. Our human bonds, as well as gospel living, require us to reach out in the daily giving of ourselves to others. We cannot give what we do not possess. Concern for our inner resources – gifts and talents – is as necessary as the sharing from our material storehouse of goods.

What are the alms we bring to others? The motto of the Little Brothers of the Poor comes to mind: "Flowers before bread." The French founder of the Little Brothers, Armand Marquiset, reached out to the suffering elderly after World War II. "Because above all people need love" motivated Marquiset to visit and deliver hot meals *with flowers* to the elderly poor in Paris. To this day those who bring nourishment to the elderly poor in the name of the Little Brothers come as friends with flowers or other gifts of beauty in their hands.

When we widen our vision to include the necessity of truly caring without calculation, we become aware of the prodigality of God's kind of loving. Learning to share what we *have* and *are* is a Godlike kind of squandering. We are not meant to hoard. We are meant to share. Human tendency to avarice and the other deadly sins is counteracted by acts of genuine care, such as the simple works of mercy.

Considerations Concerning Scruples

Ignatius suffered from scruples, which helped him to be wise in working with persons in like situations (Fleming 1992, pp. 275–279). Fleming tells us that Ignatius was troubled by scruples during his experience of conversion at Manresa (1522–1523). One can speculate that the insertions of thoughts on this matter arise from his struggles (ibid., p. 275). In his day, scruples were blamed on the devil. An old word fallen out of our religious vocabulary, a scruple is a self-imposed restraint on behavior that too rigidly inhibits certain actions. For example, one loses one's place in a prayer and must keep repeating the prayer over and over for fear of not saying it properly. Today, when such behavior is lived at an extreme we consider that the individual suffers from an obsessive-compulsive personality disorder. Scrupulosity makes us far too exacting about that which need not be taken so seriously. A more positive approach to any tendency to scrupulosity begins with looking at our emotions; especially fear, which can paralyze us. Fear can have its roots in compulsions that cause anxiety and emotional disturbance. It is important to say that if you are companioning someone on her or his spiritual journey and find that they suffer from scruples, you may want to encourage that person to seek counseling. Times of transition, change, and chaos pose the conditions that may prompt the emergence of scruples. Inner and outer circumstances cause strain to the point of guilt. The feeling of guilt can be stimulated in us at an early age, especially by underdeveloped adults who exercise power over us. Parents can teach children erroneous principles of living, for example, all expressions of self-concern are terrible, when we know that a healthy ego develops from a healthy concern for the self. Too many negative tapes played over and over again can cause breakdowns. The formation of our own conscience is essential to psychic and spiritual health. Consequently, good counseling in tandem with spiritual direction can do much to help us find our own way to inner freedom, which is, of course, the opposite of scrupulous living.

Considerations for Thinking with the Church Today

Finally, this section is the last inclusion in Ignatius's substantial final section of the Exercises (Fleming 1992, pp. 281–291). In an age when praise and reverence are words rarely used or understood, thinking with the Church is an enigma.[1] Individualism and self-serving motivations seem to be the order of the day. Ignatius loved the Church with eyes wide open to its institutional faults and the failings of its members. He was convinced that the Spirit of love always has the final word.

We seem to neither know nor recognize legitimate authority. Perhaps this is so because we do not know and exercise our own authority. The word AUTHORITY carries with it a sense of listening to who we are, how we are gifted, and what responsibilities result from this for us.[2] Respecting this gift in ourselves spills over into reverence and respect for broader authority, especially the Divine.

The Trinity is the source and giver of life, hence is the main authority concerning Life and its goals. Life carries with it all the information needed to develop each unique species. Trees, plants, vegetables, birds, animals, fish, the tides of oceans, the flow of river – all live, multiply out of what they are. The mountains are solid and strong enough to house and nourish endless kinds of life, even humans.

Humans are images of God with intellect, memory, imagination and will. Properly used and developed, these powers enable and empower us to search out our identity and purpose. Each person shows forth a different facet of the Divinity. This fact demands of us *praise* and *esteem* for all and every variety of vocation. Ignatius only mentioned single life, religious life, or married life, but within that broad area are individual expressions of talents, that is, artists, writers, musicians, poets, cooks, seamstresses, tailors, teachers, doctors, *ad infinitum*. All the colors of creation can hardly match the variety of talents latent in humans. And each has its place in the scheme of creation.

Praise, reverence, honor are strengthened by the sacramental life of the Church. Primary is the fact that the Church is a living *organism* and not an institution or corporation in the business world sense. The grass roots of the Church are people who need nourishment and find this in symbol, sacrament, community and patterns of prayer. The sacraments are meant to be living aqueducts of divine life that incorporate us with one another in a single flow, give us spiritual strength in times of illness, make us intimates with Jesus in the breaking of the bread, and heal our wounds through mercy.

Compassion in reconciliation blesses the vessels of seed-carrying life in marriage. Priests may be called as caretakers of truth through Holy Orders. Even the immensity of our human frailty has not stemmed the vitality of the pilgrim Church. Its authority is found in its divine origin and its commitment to be sustenance for those on the journey of faith. The Paschal Mystery is its heartbeat. The Church with all its weakness holds this sacred trust on earth. The Church is a living communion of individuals seeking a way home.

The teaching wing of the Church is found in its theologians, scripture scholars, and liturgists who must continually be motivated by love for the truth and the desire to preserve the faith of our ancestors. At times, they challenge our belief, our hope, and our fidelity. In turn, we must find our voice to dialogue with them, refine our and their thinking about important matters, including our relationship with the Trinity and our responsibility toward all of creation.

Above all, we want to hold fast to belief in Jesus' promise to have his Spirit with us to the end of time. The Spirit is present in the whole Church and in each of us. Pentecost was a conspiracy. In Latin, the word *conspire* literally means "to breathe with." The thinking church, the mature community of faith, is a church involved in a conspiracy with the Spirit. We are conspirers with the Holy Spirit of God. The cenacle – upper room – is an apt metaphor for the Church in our time. Is our time of confusion, anxiety, and endless uncertainty so unlike that time long ago when they huddled fearfully in the upper room, waiting in expectancy, openness, and vulnerability? I think not. So we wait with conspiring patience in the metaphorical cenacles of today, trusting the promise that the Spirit will be sent "clothing" us with a new power from on high (Luke 24:49).

What we choose to fight is so tiny!
What fights us is so great!
 . . .
When we win it's with small things,
and the triumph itself makes us small.
What is extraordinary and eternal does
not want to be bent by us . . .
Winning does not tempt . . .
This is how [we] grow: by being defeated, decisively,
by constantly greater beings.

 —Rainer Marie Rilke
  (from "The Man Watching," *Selected Poems of*
  Rainer Maria Rilke, translated by Robert Bly, 105, 107)

Notes

1. For provocative insight into thinking with the Church today, see Dick Westley, "Giving up the Faith In Order to Be Faithful" (Clendenen 2002, pp. 101–116).

2. See Robert J. Bueter, SJ, "Living the Spiritual Life with Authority" (Clendenen 2002, pp. 117–137).

Learning from Another's Life

❦

by Avis Clendenen

SISTER IRENE DUGAN'S FRIEND MURRAY STEIN CONTENDS THAT only those who have been or are being transformed can be agents of larger transformations. He says, "the transforming person is someone who realizes the inherent self to the maximum extent possible and in turn influences others to do the same" (1998, p. xxiv). Stein goes on to say that there are exceptional people in all areas of human activity, just as there are average achievers and slow learners. This applies to the affairs of psychological and spiritual growth. Not all people desire to attain the level of individuation or hunger for the soul-making inner work that makes one a transforming and transformational person. In describing this small minority, Stein says, "their lives show an extraordinary degree of uniqueness, imagination, and pristine individuality. They are leaders in the area of spiritual direction" (ibid., pp. 146–148). Irene Dugan was such a woman.

Teacher and Disciple

Little did I know that when I retrieved a box containing this manuscript from the front desk of the Cenacle that Irene had plans for the next seven years of my life! The teacher leaves a legacy with her student. The box of treasures included various articles and references to other resources, including *Parabola*, a journal Irene respected as one of the numerous multidisciplinary reference tools she used to expand her own intellectual and spiritual horizons. The term *parabola* refers to a curving line that sails outward and

returns with a new expansion. Her interest in this journal illus-
trates the breadth of Irene's inquisitiveness in exploring all avenues
of the world's wisdom traditions to mine meaning for contemporary life. I reacquainted myself with the journal and discovered
that its mission and vision seemed resonant with Irene. The pro-
motional materials for the premier issue of *Parabola* state the conviction that human experience is significant, that life essentially
makes sense in spite of our confusions, that human beings are not
here on earth by accident but for a purpose, and that whatever that
purpose may be, it means we are born for the quest of discovering
meaning and identity. In my efforts to probe more deeply the multiple venues that influenced Irene, I found some insight into the
legacy I inherited from her and the tasks that awaited my attention
after her death.

The teacher/student, spiritual mentor/disciple relationship is
unique. J. L. Walker, in "An Essential Commitment" (2000), dis-
cusses the interdependency of the quest for learning and devotion
to realization that ignites the dynamic in this kind of special relationship. The teacher claims the calling when a student appears.
The spiritual guide can only set forth a path if the disciple is willing to walk. When the student-disciple arrives before the teacher-
mentor and both cross the threshold of each other with openness,
trust, reverence, and devotion to the deeper truths, then the way
opens and realization is possible. The second-century C.E. Indian
Buddhist sage Nagarjuna left the following direction to a novice
seeking a spiritual guide:

> Devote yourself to one possessing twelve qualities:
> Much learning and great wisdom,
> Not aspiring for material goods or possessions,
> Possessing the Spirit of Awakening and great compassion,
> Enduring hardships and having little depression or fatigue,
> Having great practical advice, liberated from the mundane path,
> And possessing knowledge and erudition
>   and comprehension of the signs of warmth
> [Indication of success in spiritual practice].
> (quoted in Walker 2000, p. 40)

When an authentic meeting of the two has occurred and a climate of attunement born, the spiritual teacher and disciple begin a shared journey. Spiritually speaking, their finding one another is not an accident or fate but recognition that they have been part of each other's spiritual destiny all along. The spiritual mentor imparts her or his very being to the disciple – not merely knowledge, no matter how penetrating or profound (ibid., pp. 40, 42). It is as though they possess the same key that opens the door to the Way. Christian theology might refer to this most sacred of relationships as an occasion of grace. Intimate relationships of this kind, as with all truly intimate relationships, become the richest environments for psychological and spiritual transformation.

Ignatius of Loyola and Ira Progoff became such inner guides for others, occasions of grace. As Irene stated in the introduction, Ignatius could have been a twentieth-century holistic depth psychologist and Ira Progoff a sixteenth-century spiritual visionary. Each discovered keys to the ways of becoming a wise old man and a wise old woman and chose to share those discoveries with others. Their respective legacies include the founding of the Society of Jesus, a religious community dedicated to the Spiritual Exercises of St. Ignatius among other ministries, and the founding of the *Intensive Journal*® method and Dialogue House, headquartered in New York and now under the direction of Jonathon Progoff, Ira's son. Irene Dugan found in Ignatius and Ira the twelve qualities of the great teacher and, in her own way, extended their lifework through her own.

It is evident to me today that the first quarter century of my relationship with Sister Irene Dugan was essential preparation for the past seven years since her departure from this side of the great divide. These years have disclosed the sometimes-thin veil that separates us in the apparent finality of physical presence we call death. While there is nothing so loud as the silence of death, it is a doorway to the experience of limitless presence, if we remain expectant, open, and vulnerable.

A Cenacle Sister reflecting on Irene recently said to me, "Irene's life was lived on a larger than personal level." Irene often spoke with me of a living beyond ego. This insight suggested an interior balance

that emerges in working with one's inner world and its outer manifestations. Her largesse of spirit permeates the present. The disciple
finishes some aspect of the teacher's unfinished lifework. This is part
of the unspoken knowing from the beginning. Transformational
relationships ultimately evoke new horizons to be explored and new
avenues of effort and work (Stein 1998, pp. 99–100).

> *They whom we love and lose are no longer where they were before.*
> *They are now wherever we are.*
>
> —St. John Chrysostom

While the focus of this book has been on the individual quest for
greater authenticity, spiritual depth, and self-realization, Irene recognized the essential interplay of the personal and social, the private and public spheres. Taking initiative in and responsibility for
one's own inner life and the challenges of personal psychospiritual
growth invariably has an impact on the world. Jesus preached a
kingdom that comes within first and then moves outward toward
the transformation of no less than the world itself. Toward the end
of his life, C. G. Jung stressed that only if enough individuals commit themselves totally to taking responsibility for their own consciousness, each invested in her or his quest for wholeness, can the
world survive catastrophe.

Irene Dugan dedicated her lifework to evoking and provoking an
urgency in others regarding the quest for human and spiritual
wholeness, facing our limits and possibilities, infinite potentialities
and terrorizing finitude, working with the light and shadow within
each human personality, and embracing the mysteries and miseries
of the pilgrimage we call life. In a time such as ours we must be vig-
ilant in seeking those few among us who possess the ancient sage's
twelve qualities: (1) much learning and (2) great wisdom, (3) not
aspiring for material goods or possessions, (4) possessing the Spirit
of Awakening and (5) great compassion, (6) enduring hardships and
(7) having little depression or fatigue, (8) having great practical
advice, (9) liberated from the mundane path, and (10) possessing

knowledge and (11) erudition, and (12) comprehension of the signs of warmth [an indication of success in spiritual practice]. These are the holy ones to whom we owe our allegiance and devotion, for surely they will guide our feet onto the pathways of peace.

This book is the fruition of many decades of Irene's lifework and my effort to attune myself to her so that together we could "extend" the work of the triumvirate of Ignatius, Progoff, and Dugan. Irene Dugan believed it necessary to learn the Progoff *Intensive Journal*® method as a pure process prior to applying aspects of Progoff's insights to the Ignatian spiritual path.[1] In essence, then, Irene engaged in a life-study of St. Ignatius. Over the span of many decades, she carefully examined the cycles in Ignatius's life, attempting to discern Ignatius's own inner work in devising and designing the Spiritual Exercises, which is part of the legacy Ignatius bequeathed to those who follow him. Thus, Irene's effort to extend the work of Ignatius and Progoff created the fresh combination of insight and processes, of which this book is its product.

Learning from Another's Life

In 1983, Ira Progoff published his last book, *Life-Study: Experiencing Creative Lives by the Intensive Journal*® *Method*. Progoff brought this work to fruition after years of studying how people go through the process of negotiating the joys and concerns, defeats and triumphs in their given lives. He was interested in why it was that some people thrived through adversity, becoming richer and fuller personalities, and others, experiencing similar obstacles, emerged with personas of burdened victims. He studied the lives of high profile, publicly acknowledged creative people throughout history to find out what was involved in their creative productivity. Progoff adapted his *Intensive Journal*® methods to provide a way to give studied attention to another's completed life and by doing so uncover messages for our own life today. When one's life is over in the physical sense, that life can become a source of new creativity for those who become attuned to it (Progoff 1983, p. 15). One may begin as an outsider to the life of a wisdom figure who has died, but by slowly gaining an inner sense of their achievements, struggles, plans, and goals – the chronos and kairos of another's life – one gains access to broader perspectives on the changes to be anticipated in living a life span, closer contact with the reality of the interplay of light and shadow in the creative personality and its respective processes, and a new vantage point from which to examine the fundamental values that guide a richly lived life (see Progoff 1983, pp. 23–46).

Being a Trustee

In choosing to engage Progoff's insights into learning from another's life one becomes, in his words, a journal trustee. It is a decision to hold another in sacred trust because somehow you sense that something in the experiences through which they lived contains a message for you. Life-Study is a choice to enter a life not your own in order to participate in the cycles of achievement and frustration through which they passed.

Progoff says, "As a work of art can do, a human life can continue and extend its creativity through the persons who re-enter and re-experience its meaning ... the experiences that it can still evoke and can bring into the world by its stimulating effects have not been exhausted. These may, indeed, be illimitable and have no end" (ibid., p. 15).

As a trustee, you are working with another's life rather than your own. Being a trustee requires empathy. It is not a diagnostic exercise. One tries to reexperience the life of another from that person's point of view and not one's own. One gives studied attention and attunement to another in order to work into and through another's life without dissecting or analyzing the subject of the life-study. One marshals the virtues of trust, honor, and integrity as one approaches the life of another as if crossing a threshold into sacred territory.

Life-Study and Sister Irene Dugan

I am indebted to Dr. Joyce Kemp, r.c., a Sister of the Cenacle who was mentored by Irene Dugan, r.c., and is a certified Progoff *Intensive Journal*® workshop leader, who led me through the processes of Life-Study and learning from another's life in a weekend workshop. My original intent had been to conclude this final chapter with journal entries made during my work on Sister Irene Dugan's life in the workshop. Early on in the weekend, I realized that I could not publish what I recorded as I crossed the threshold into Irene's life from the outside in. I was reawakened to the wisdom of Irene's consistent admonition not to share in print what one has written in the privacy of one's journal. She always cautioned her directees to reveal verbally whatever one wanted to share in the trusted confidence of the mentor-disciple relationship, but not to hand over one's private journal writing to anybody. Irene shredded all her personal correspondence and journals prior to her death. Experiencing myself as a trustee of this book and working with Sister Joyce Kemp, it became clear that I could not print the outcomes of my meditations and musings. The insights that emerged through reentering the scope and depth of Sister Irene Dugan's life are messages for me alone to hold and honor.

Also in this regard, a memory surfaced while doing the Progoff workshop on Life-Study with Irene's life, which reinforced this decision. When I returned home from the weekend workshop I replayed a videotape of one of the famous interviews with C. G. Jung near the end of his life (d. 1961). The interviewer asked Jung if he had ever shared his dreams and been analyzed by Sigmund Freud. Jung answered yes and said that Freud in turn had shared some of his dreams with Jung to seek Jung's interpretation. The interviewer's interest was immediately piqued by this disclosure, and he asked Jung to elaborate on what Freud shared with him. Jung hesitated and then stammered for a time, finally saying that such an inquiry was quite "indiscreet." The interviewer countered by reminding Jung that Freud had been dead for more than twenty years; surely he could enlighten the world now? Again Jung paused and then said, "These regards last longer than life. I prefer not to talk." I was impressed by Jung's sense of professional ethics and the clarity of his conviction that our lives last longer than the life itself. Being discreet is an almost lost art.

Thus, I exercise the art of discretion and conclude this book with a peek into the process and an encouragement to the reader to participate in the official Dialogue House Life-Study work-

shop entitled "Learning from Another's Life."[2] Being a trustee of
the book you hold in your hands has been an extraordinary experience of the privilege and pain of working in another's life for
the empathic understandings that emerge when we enter another's life flow, falling into the stream of what moved her, imaginatively being where she once was.

Colloquy with Irene

As you are now aware, having traveled through this book, the colloquy or inner dialogue is a central feature of Ignatian spirituality
and the holistic depth psychology of Ira Progoff. There is a point
some way into the Life-Study process when you engage the subject
of your study in a colloquy. In this session you are invited to meet
in direct relationship with the person with whom you have been
working as a journal trustee (see Progoff 1983, pp. 241–248). Progoff
creates the mood of this session by telling you that it is as though
"you are sitting side by side with her in an atmosphere in which
each can speak with freedom and without reserve. It is our opportunity to discuss all that has been building within us" (ibid., p. 243).

The following is a brief excerpt from my Colloquy with Irene on
February 2, 2003:

> Irene: (a brilliant smile)
>
> Me: (a more brilliant smile)
>
> Irene: We did it!
>
> Me: Took me longer than my whole doctoral education!
>
> Irene (enjoying my phony incredulity): We are doing something
> here that is important, Avis. The book itself isn't really that impor-
> tant. It's what has happened in the doing of it all. What has hap-
> pened to you, for you, in you . . . your awareness of what it means
> to be in and speak from the majority of your life? Now you know
> what I meant when I told you that you needed to be in the major-
> ity of your life to understand the inner world and its workings.
>
> Me: And you think I understand these matters now?

Irene: Ah, "these matters live longer than life" – you liked that line from Jung. Me too. I think you heard him say this because it was a confirmation of your working with my life now that I am gone. This is a subtle kind of thinking about life that is important for you now . . .

This dialogue went back and forth for a good half hour and numerous written pages. It was reminiscent of our dialogues within the context of spiritual direction. I found myself getting lost in the exchange and losing a self-consciousness about the exercise. Sometimes I talked at length and other times Irene took the floor with relish and in her own inimitable way. There were hesitations. Quiet pauses. Some emotion. I recorded everything that seemed to come out of the pen and onto the paper. When I finished, I closed the journal, shook my hands, which were stiff from the concentrated writing, got up and took a walk to mull over the experience. There is so much more to know about another's life and so much that must be entrusted to mystery. "These regards last longer than life." The relationship established or extended between the covers of a journal is an open invitation both to know more and to the mystery.

Accomplishing One's Death

Literally hours before her death on July 21, 1997, a nurse entered Irene's room to give her an injection for pain. It was reported to me that Irene gestured for the nurse to stop. She knew that the medication would dull her senses to what was happening within and around her. True to character, she indicated her desire not to be sedated in the now of her dying by simply saying to the nurse, "No, please, I want to have the experience." It was also shared with me that in her final hours she whispered to a friend at her bedside, "I can't believe this is really happening." For those among us with gusto and courage for living large, separation from the good and beautiful is difficult.[3]

Irene's final wafting was a wrenching away from the life she so loved living. And like her living, she died having the experience. Carl Jung once said that we should accomplish our individual deaths. I think he meant that if we are blessed with a long life, we come to death having already touched heaven. By living large, in consciousness, with zest and gratitude, we live life to the full and thus eternity, in the really real sense, is not found on the other side of death but is all around us in the disguise of now.

> *I love the dark hours of my being*
> *in which my senses drop into the deep.*
> *I have found in them, as in old letters,*
> *my private life, that is already lived through,*
> *and become wide and powerful now, like legends.*
> *Then I know that there is room in me*
> *for a second huge and timeless life.*
>
> —Rainer Marie Rilke
> (from "I Am Too Alone In The World," in
> *Ten Poems by Rainer Maria Rilke,*
> translated by Robert Bly, p. 4)

Notes

1. For more information about *Intensive Journal*® workshops and seminars, contact Dialogue House Associates, 799 Broadway, Suite 519, New York, New York, 10003, (212) 673-5880, (800) 221-5844, e-mail: infor@intensivejournal.org, or visit the Web site at www.intensivejournal.org.

2. For specific information about the Life-Study *Intensive Journal*® workshop "Learning from Another's Life," contact Dialogue House Associates.

3. For further insight in this regard, see Mary Ann Bergfeld, RSM, "Irene Dugan – Her Life Was a Song" (Clendenen 2002, pp. 1–5).

Significant Dates in the Life
of Sister Irene Dugan, r.c.

December 4, 1909 Born in New York City, the eldest of nine children of Thomas Dugan and Irene McBride Dugan

September 8, 1930 Entered the Religious of the Cenacle in Lake Ronkonkoma, New York

June 2, 1938 Perpetual profession of vows

September 1938 Ministry at the Cenacle in Boston

June 1943 One of the founders of the Cenacle in Milwaukee, Wisconsin

January 1956 Ministry at the Carmichael Cenacle in Sacramento, California

February 1963 Ministry at the Longwood Cenacle in Chicago

1970 Began training and giving Progoff *Intensive Journal*® workshops in the United States and Europe

1973 Founded with Paul Robb, SJ, the Spiritual Direction Institute in collaboration with the Jesuit School of Theology in Chicago

Appointed adjunct faculty in spiritual direction training at the Jesuit School of Theology in Chicago

1981 Sabbatical in LaLouvesc, France, birthplace of the Congregation of the Cenacle

1983 Appointed scholar in residence at the Institute of Pastoral Studies, Loyola University, Chicago

1987 Doctor of Humane Letters, *honoris causa*, from Loyola University, Chicago

1988 Resided at the Fullerton Cenacle in Chicago and continued to write and teach

1996 Began ministry with local youth from the Chicago area

July 21, 1997	Died in Chicago
August 25, 1998	The Sister Irene Dugan Alternative Public High School opened in Chicago for youth at risk
July 20, 2002	"In Remembrance: A Celebration of the Life and Spiritual Legacy of Sister Irene Dugan, r.c.", and the publication of *Spirituality in Depth: Essays in Honor of Sister Irene Dugan, r.c.* (Chiron Publications)
2004	Publication of *Love Is All Around in Disguise: Meditations for Spiritual Seekers* (Chiron Publications)

List of Works Cited

Adam, David. 1987. *The Cry of the Deer: Meditations on the Hymn of St. Patrick*. Wilton, Conn.: Morehouse-Barlow.

Baldwin, Christina. 1990. *Life's Companion: Journal Writing as a Spiritual Quest*. New York: Bantam Books.

Brueggemann, Walter. 2000. *Texts That Linger, Words That Explode: Listening to Prophetic Voices*. Minneapolis: Fortress Press.

Buber, Martin. 1996. *Ministry of Money*. No. 103 (August).

Cahill, Thomas. 1995. *How the Irish Saved Civilization: The Untold Story of Ireland's Heroic Role from the Fall of Rome to the Rise of Medieval Europe*. New York: Doubleday.

Clare, of Assisi, Saint. 1988. *Clare of Assisi: Early Documents*. Regis Armstrong, trans. New York: Paulist Press.

Clendenen, Avis, ed. 2002. *Spirituality in Depth: Essays in Honor of Sister Irene Dugan, r.c.* Wilmette, IL.: Chiron Publications.

Daniels, David, and Helen Palmer. 2003. "Introduction to the Enneagram," at www.authenticenneagram.com.

Eckhart, Meister. 1987. *Sermons and Treatises*, vol. 1. M.O. Walshe, trans. and ed. Boston: Element Books.

Egan, Harvey D., SJ. 1980. "The devout Christian of tomorrow will be a mystic": Mysticism and Karl Rahner's theology. In William J. Kelly, ed., *Theology and Discovery: Essays in Honor of Karl Rahner, SJ*. Milwaukee: Marquette University Press.

Eigo, Francis, O.S.A. 1994. *All Generations Shall Call Me Blessed*. Villanova, Pa.: The Villanova University Press.

Eliot, T. S. 1971. *The Complete Poems and Plays (1909–1950)*. New York: Harcourt Brace and Company.

Endean, Philip. 2001. *Karl Rahner and Ignatian Spirituality*. New York: Oxford University Press.

Fleming, David L., SJ. 1996. *Draw Me into Your Friendship: A Literal Translationand Contemporary Reading of the Spiritual Exercises*. Saint Louis, Mo.: The Institute of Jesuit Sources.

Goleman, Daniel. 1985. *Vital Lies, Simple Truths: The Psychology of Self-Deception*. New York: Simon and Schuster.

Hopkins, Gerard Manley. 1952. *Poems of Gerard Manley Hopkins*. London: Oxford University Press.

Hudson, Joyce Rockwood. 2000. *Natural Spirituality: Recovering the Wisdom Tradition in Christianity*. Danielsville, Ga.: JRH Publications.

Jegen, Carol Frances, B.V.M., ed. 1985. *Mary According to Women*. New York: Paulist Press.

Johnson, Robert A. 1991. *Owning Your Own Shadow: Understanding the Dark Side of the Psyche*. San Francisco: Harper Collins Publishers.

————. 1998. *Balancing Heaven and Earth: A Memoir of Visions, Dreams, and Realizations*. San Francisco: Harper Collins.

Jung, C. G. 1931. Marriage as a psychological relationship. In *CW*, vol. 17. Princeton, N.J.: Princeton University Press, 1954.

————. 1946. Psychotherapy and a philosophy of life. In *CW*, vol. 16. Princeton, N.J.: Princeton University Press, 1954, 1966.

————. 1950. Concerning mandala symbolism. In *CW*, vol. 9i. Princeton, N.J.: Princeton University Press, 1959, 1968.

————. 1952. Answer to Job. In *CW*, vol. 11. Princeton, N.J.: Princeton University Press, 1958, 1969.

————. 1992. *Letters, Vol.1: 1906–1950*. R. F. C. Hull and Gerhard Adler, trans. Princeton, N.J.: Princeton University Press.

Keen, Sam. 1970. *To a Dancing God*. New York: Harper and Row.

Laing, R. D. 1970. *Knots*. New York: Pantheon Books.

L'Engle, Madeleine. 1988. *Two-Part Invention: The Story of a Marriage*. San Francisco: Harper Collins Publishers.

Logue, Christopher. 1996. *Selected Poems*. London: Faber and Faber.

Luce, William. 1976. *The Belle of Amherst: A Play Based on the Life of Emily Dickinson*. Boston: Houghton Mifflin.

May, Gerald. 1982. *Will and Spirit*. San Francisco: Harper and Row.

McCool, Gerald, ed. 1975. *A Rahner Reader*. New York: Seabury Press.

McGuire, William, and R.F.C. Hull, eds. *C.G. Jung Speaking: Interviews and Encounters*. Princeton, N.J.: Princeton University Press.

McKenna, Bernard. 1929. *The Dogma of the Immaculate Conception*. Washington, D.C.: U.S. Catholic Bishops.

Moore, Sebastian. 1990–91. Jesus the liberator of desire. *CrossCurrents* 40/4:477–498.

Nouwen, Henri. 1994. *Our Greatest Gift: A Meditation on Dying and Caring*. New York: Harper Collins.

O'Malley, William J., SJ. 1996. *The Fifth Week*. Chicago: Loyola University Press.

O'Neal, Norman, SJ. 2000. A biography of Ignatius Loyola. http://maple.lemoyne.edu/-bucko/v_ignat.

Oxford Book of Carols. New York: Oxford University Press, 1964.

Palmer, Parker. 2000. *Let Your Life Speak: Listening to the Voice of Vocation*. San Francisco: Jossey-Boss, Inc.

Patterson, Margot. 2001. Chivalry inspired by a courtier saint. *National Catholic Reporter* 37/24:15.

Peck, M. Scott. 1978. *The Road Less Traveled: A New Psychology of Love, Traditional Values and Spiritual Growth*. New York: Simon and Schuster.

Progoff, Ira. 1959. *Depth Psychology and Modern Man*. New York: McGraw-Hill Book Company.

_____. 1971. *The Star Cross: An Entrance Meditation*. New York: Dialogue House Library.

_____. 1980. *The Practice of Process Meditation*. New York: Dialogue House Library.

_____. 1983. *Life-Study: Experiencing Creative Lives by the Intensive Journal®
Method*. New York: Dialogue House Library.

_____. 1985. *The Dynamics of Hope: Perspectives of Process in Anxiety and
Creativity, Imagery and Dreams*. New York: Dialogue House Library.

_____. 1992. *At a Journal Workshop: Writing to Access the Power of the
Unconscious and Evoke Creative Ability*. Rev. ed. Los Angeles: Jeremy P.
Tarcher. Rev. ed. Originally published: New York: Penguin Putnam, 1975.

Rahner, Hugo, trans. 1960. *Saint Ignatius Loyola: Letters to Women*. New York:
Herder.

Rahner, Karl, SJ. 1963. *Mary, Mother of the Lord*. New York: Herder and Herder.

_____. 1969a. *Hearers of the Word*. New York: Seabury Press.

_____. 1969b. *Theological Investigations*. Vol. 6. London: Darton, Longman,
and Todd, Ltd.

_____. 1969c. *Grace in Freedom*. New York: Herder and Herder.

_____. 1996. *The Great Church Year*. New York: Crossroads.

Richo, David. 2001. *Mary Within: A Jungian Contemplation of Her Titles and
Powers*. New York: Crossroad Publishing Co.

_____. 2003. *Wisdom's Way: Quotations for Meditation*. Private Distribution
Online: davericho.com.

Rilke, Rainer Maria. 1934. *Letters to a Young Poet*. M. D. Herter Norton, trans.
New York: W. W. Norton and Co.

_____. 1981. *I Am Too Alone In The World: Ten Poems by Rainer Maria Rilke*.
Robert Bly, trans. New York: The Silver Hands Press.

_____. 1981. *Selected Poems of Rainer Maria Rilke*. Robert Bly, trans. New York:
Harper & Row.

_____. 1996. *Rilke's Book of Hours: Love Poems to God*. Anita Barrows and
Joanna Macy, trans. New York: Riverhead Books.

Saint Ignatius of Loyola. 1959. *Letters of St. Ignatius of Loyola*. William J. Young,
trans. Chicago: Loyola University Press.

Sanford, John. 1984. *The Invisible Partners: How the Male and Female in Each of
Us Affects Our Relationships*. Mahwah, N.J.: Paulist Press.

_____. 1987. *The Kingdom Within*. San Francisco: Harper and Row.

_____. 1993. *Jung and the Problem of Evil: The Strange Trial of Dr. Hyde.* Boston: Sigo Press.

Searcy, Edwin, ed. 2003. *Awed to Heaven, Rooted in Earth: Prayers of Walter Brueggmann.* Minneapolis: Fortress Press.

Stein, Murray. 1996. *Practicing Wholeness.* New York: Continuum Publishing Company.

_____. 1998a. *Jung's Map of the Soul.* Chicago: Open Court.

_____. 1998b. *Transformation: Emergence of the Self.* College Station, Texas: A&M University Press.

Stroud, Joanne H. 1994. *The Bonding of Will and Desire.* New York: Continuum Publishing Company.

Teilhard de Chardin, Pierre. 1961. *Hymn of the Universe.* New York: Harper and Row.

The Complete Parallel Bible: New Revised Standard Version, Revised English Bible New American Bible, and the New Jerusalem Bible. 1993. New York: Oxford University Press.

Thich Nhat Hanh. 1975. *The Miracle of Mindfulness: A Manual on Meditation.* Boston: Beacon Press.

Tillich, Paul. 1952. *The Courage to Be.* New Haven, CT: Yale University Press.

_____. 1963. *The Eternal Now.* New York: Charles Scribner's Sons.

Thorald, Alger, trans. 1943. *The Dialogues of Catherine of Siena.* Westminster, Md.: The Newman Bookshop.

Trible, Phyllis. 1978. *God and the Rhetoric of Sexuality.* Philadelphia: Fortress Press.

Walker, J. L. 2000. An essential commitment. *Parabola* 25/3:39–43. Denville, N.J.: The Society for the Study of Myth and Tradition.

Suggested Reading

Angelou, Maya. 1993. *Wouldn't Take Nothing for My Journey Now.* New York: Random House.

Auden, W. H. 1945. *The Collected Poetry of W. H. Auden.* New York: Random House.

Bachelard, Gaston. 1969. *The Poetics of Reverie.* Daniel Russell, trans. New York: The Orion Press.

Bateson, Mary Catherine. 1989. *Composing a Life.* New York: Atlantic Monthly Press.

Beckett, Wendy. 1993. *The Gaze of Love.* San Francisco: Harper Collins.

Bernardin, Joseph Cardinal. 1997. *The Gift of Peace.* Chicago: Loyola Press.

Bhagavad Gita. New York: Holt, Rinehart and Winston, 1968.

Binchy, Maeve. 1991. *The Lilac Bus.* New York: Delacorte Press.

Bolen, Jean Shinoda. 1995. *Crossing to Avalon.* San Francisco: Harper Collins.

Boulet, Susan Seddon. 1989. *Shaman, The Paintings of Susan Seddon Boulet.* San Francisco: Pomegranate Artbooks.

Breathnach, Sarah. 1995. *Simple Abundance.* New York: Warner Books.

Brodrick, James. 1956. *St. Ignatius Loyola: The Pilgrim Year.* New York: Farrar Straus and Cudahy.

Browning, Elizabeth Barrett. 1954. *Sonnets from the Portuguese.* New York: Doubleday.

Buchan, Alice. 1948. *Joan of Arc and the Recovery of France.* London: Hodder and Stoughton.

Carse, James P. 1995. *Breakfast at the Victory*. San Francisco: Harper Collin.

_____. 1995. *The Silence of God*. San Francisco: Harper Collins.

Carson, Rachel. 1956. *The Sense of Wonder*. New York: Harper and Row.

Catherine of Siena. 1943. *The Dialogues of Catherine of Siena*. Algar Thorold, trans. Westminister, Md.: The Newman Bookshop.

Chaucer, Geoffrey. 1932. *Troilus and Cressida*. George Philip Krapp, ed. New York: Random House.

Clancy, Thomas H. 1978. *The Conversational Word of God: A Commentary on the Doctrine of St. Ignatius of Loyola*. St Louis, Mo.: The Institute of Jesuit Sources.

Coates, Cecilia. 1996. Plugging in. *Common Boundary*. September/October, pp. 24–31.

Csikszentmihalyi, Mihaly. 1990. *Flow: The Psychology of Optimal Experience*. New York: Harper and Row.

cummings, e. e. 1965. *A Selection of Poems*. New York: Harcourt, Brace and World.

Dass, Ram, and Paul Gorman. 1988. *How Can I Help?* New York: Alfred A. Knopf.

de Castillejo, Irene Claremont. 1990. *Knowing Women, A Feminine Psychology*. Boston: Shambhala.

de Chardin, Pierre Teilhard. 1965. *Building the Earth*. Noel Lindsay, trans. Wilkes Barre: Dimension Book.

_____. 1960. *The Divine Milieu*. New York: Harper and Row.

_____. 1961. *Hymn of the Universe*. New York: Harper and Row.

de Saint Exupery, Antoine. 1943. *The Little Prince*. New York: Harcourt, Brace.

Dickens, Charles. 1971. *A Christmas Carol*. New York: New York Public Library.

_____. 1995. *David Copperfield*. New York: North-South Books.

_____. 1994. *Great Expectations*. New York: Barnes and Noble.

Dickinson, Emily. 1960. *The Complete Poems of Emily Dickinson*. Thomas H. Johnson, ed. Boston: Little, Brown and Company.

Dourley, John P. 1987. *Love, Celibacy and the Inner Marriage.* Toronto: Inner City Books.

Drabble, Margaret. 1987. *The Radiant Way.* New York: Viking Penguin.

Dunn, Claire. 2000. *Carl Jung: Wounded Healer of the Soul: An Illustrated Biography.* New York: Parabola Books.

Dunne, John S. 1990. The ways of desire. *Cross Currents* 40/4 (Winter, 1990–91).

Eadie, Betty J. 1996. *The Awakening Heart.* New York: Simon and Schuster.

Eliade, Mircea. 1982. *Imagination and Meaning.* New York: Seabury Press.

Emerson, Ralph Waldo. 1996. *Self-Reliance: The Wisdom of Ralph Waldo Emerson as Inspiration for Daily Living.* New York: Bell Tower.

Estes, Clarissa Pinkola. 1992. *Women Who Run with the Wolves.* New York: Ballantine Books.

Evans, Nicholas. 1995. *The Horse Whisperer.* New York: Bantam Doubleday Dell.

Field, Joanna. 1936. *A Life of One's Own.* London: Chatto and Windus. Reprinted Los Angeles: J. P. Tarcher, 1981.

Fine, Elsa H. 1973. *The Afro-American Artist.* New York: Holt, Rinehart and Winston.

Fitzgerald, F. Scott. 1996. *The Great Gatsby.* New York: Chelsea House.

Flinders, Carol Lee. 1993. *Enduring Grace.* San Francisco: Harper Collins.

Flinders, Carol Lee and Laurel Robertson. 1986. *Laurel's Kitchen.* Berkeley, Calif.: Ten Speed Press.

Frank, Anne. 1972. *The Diary of Anne Frank.* New York: Washington Square Press.

French, R. M., tr. 1960. *The Way of a Pilgrim.* London: S.P.C.K.

Fromm, Erich. 1962. *The Art of Loving.* New York: Bantam Harper and Row.

Frost, Robert. 1962. *The Poetry of Robert Frost.* Edward C. Lathem, ed. New York: Rinehart and Winston.

Gardner, Helen. 1959. *Art Through the Ages.* New York: Harcourt Brace and World.

Gibran, Kahlil. 1970. *The Prophet.* New York: Alfred A. Knopf.

Gillette, Douglas and Robert Moore. *King, Warrior, Magician, Lover.* San Francisco: Harper Collins.

Godwin, Gail. 1985. *The Finishing School.* New York: Viking.

Goldsmith, Joel S. 1986. *Practicing the Presence.* San Francisco: Harper and Row.

Greenberg, Joanne (Hannah Green). 1986. *I Never Promised You a Rose Garden.* New York: New American Library.

Grisanti, Mary Lee. 1983. *The Art of the Vatican.* New York: Excalibur Books.

Grudin, Robert. 1996. *On Dialogue.* Boston: Houghton Mifflin.

Guare, John. 1994. *Six Degrees of Separation: A Play.* New York: Random House/Vantage Books.

Hanh, Thich Nhat. 1990. *Present Moment, Wonderful Moment: Mindfulness Verses for Daily Living.* Berkeley, Calif.: Parallax Press.

_____. 1988. *The Pine Gate.* Vo Dinh Mai and Mobi Ho, trans. Fredonia, N.Y.: White Pine Press.

Hart, Thomas N. 1980. *The Art of Christian Listening.* Ramsey, N.J.: Paulist Press.

Heilbrun, Carolyn G. 1988. *Writing a Woman's Life.* New York: Ballantine Books.

Hemingway, Ernest. 1952. *The Old Man and the Sea.* New York: Charles Scribner.

Himes, Michael. 1995. *Doing the Truth in Love.* Ramsey, N.J.: Paulist Press.

Hirsch, Edward. 1996. A poetry that matters. Interview with Wislawa Szymborska. *The New York Times Magazine,* December 1, sec. 6.

Huxley, Laura Archer. 1986. *You Are Not the Target.* Los Angeles: J. P. Tarcher.

Jackson, Robert, ed. 1953. *Beautiful Gardens of the World.* London: Evand Brothers.

Jaffe, Aniela (ed.). 1979. *C.G. Jung: Word and Image.* New York: Princeton/Bollingen Series/2.

Johnson, Elizabeth. 1994. Between the times. *Review for Religious.* January/February.

Johnson, Robert. 1989. *He.* New York: Harper and Row.

_____. 1989. *She.* New York: Harper and Row.

Johnston, William. 1978. *The Inner Eye of Love*. New York: Harper and Row.

_____. 1975. *Silent Music*. New York: Harper and Row.

Judson, Alexander Corbine. 1945. The faerie queen. *The Works of Edmund Spenser*. Baltimore: The Johns Hopkins Press.

Keen, Sam. 1991. *Fire in the Belly, On Being a Man*. New York: Bantam.

_____. 1992. *The Passionate Life*. San Francisco: Harper Collins.

Kelly, Carole Marie. 1988. *Symbols of Inner Truth*. New York: Paulist Press.

Kenyon, Jane. 1990. *Let Evening Come*. St. Paul, Minn.: Graywolf Press.

Khayam, Omar. 1985. *Rubaiyat of Omar Khayam*. London: Harrap.

Kubler-Ross, Elisabeth. 1993. *On Death and Dying*. New York: Macmillan.

LaClotte, Michel, et al. 1984. *A Day in the Country*. Los Angeles: Los Angeles County Museum of Art.

_____. 1986. *Musee d'Orsay Impressionist and Post-Impressionist Masterpieces*. London: Thames and Hudson.

LaVerdiere, Eugene. 1996. *Dining at the Table of the Kingdom*. Chicago: Liturgy Training Publications.

Lawrence, Brother. 1991. *Practice the Presence of God*. Wheaton, Ill.: Harold Shaw.

L'Engle, Madeleine. 1989. *An Acceptable Time*. New York: Farrar, Straus, Giroux.

Lessing, Doris. 1983. *The Diary of a Good Neighbour*. New York: Alfred A. Knopf.

_____. 1983. *The Summer Before the Dark*. New York: Vintage Books.

Lewis, C. S. 1994. *The Chronicles of Narnia*. 3 vols. New York: Harper Collins.

_____. 1960. *The Four Loves*. San Diego: Harcourt Brace Jovanovich.

_____. 1984. *Grief Observed*. New York: Phoenix Press.

_____. 1947. *Miracles*. New York: Macmillan.

_____. 1956. *Till We Have Faces*. San Diego: Harcourt Brace Jovanovich.

Lindbergh, Anne Morrow. 1975. *Gift from the Sea*. New York: Pantheon Books.

Loyola, St. Ignatius. 1583. *The Autobiography of St. Ignatius Loyola*. Joseph F. O'Callaghan and John C. On, tr. New York: Harper and Row, 1974.

Luke, Helen M. 1989. *Dark Wood to White Rose: Journey and Transformation in Dante's Divine Comedy.* New York: Parabola Books.

_____. 1992. *Kaleidoscope: The Way of Women.* New York: Parabola Books.

_____. 1987. *Old Age.* New York: Parabola Books.

Mascetti, Manuela Dunn, ed. 1996. *Haiku, the Poetry of Zen.* New York: Hyperion.

_____. 1996. *Koans, the Lessons of Zen.* New York: Hyperion.

_____. 1996. *Sayings, the Wisdom of Zen.* New York: Hyperion.

May, Rollo. 1975. *The Courage to Create.* New York: W. W. Norton.

_____. 1969. *Love and Will.* New York: W. W. Norton.

McCarthy, Mary. 1959. *The Stones of Florence.* New York: Harcourt, Brace.

Merton, Thomas. 1970. *The Wisdom of the Desert.* New York: New Directions.

Millay, Edna St. Vincent. 1956. *Collected Poems.* San Francisco: Harper and Row.

Milton, John. 1951. "Il Peneroso." *Poems of John Milton.* New York: Harcourt, Brace.

Moore, Brian. 1972. *Catholics.* London: Jonathon Cape. Reprinted Triad/Granada, 1983.

Myss, Caroline. 1996. *The Anatomy of the Spirit: The Seven Stages of Power and Healing.* New York: Harmony Books.

Painter, Nell Irvin. 1996. *Sojouner Truth, A Life, A Symbol.* New York: W. W. Norton.

Pieper, Josef. 1954. *Leisure, The Basis of Culture.* New York: Pantheon Books.

Progoff, Ira. 1959. *Depth Psychology and Modern Man.* New York: McGraw-Hill Paperback, 1973. Reprinted by arrangement with Julian Press.

_____. 1973. *Jung, Synchronicity and Human Destiny.* New York: Delta Books.

_____. 1979. *The White Robed Monk.* New York: Dialogue House Library.

_____. 1983. *The Practice of Process Meditation.* New York: Dialogue House Library.

_____. 1992. *The Well and the Cathedral.* New York: Dialogue House.

_____. Creativity and Spirit in History and Today. Tape. New York: Dialogue House Library.

_____. The Next Step in Social Responsibility. Tape. New York: Dialogue House Library.

_____. The Star/Cross. Tape. New York: Dialogue House Library.

_____. The Will and the Cathedral. Tape. New York: Dialogue House Library.

_____. The White Robed Monk. Tape. New York: Dialogue House Library.

Rahner, Karl. 1993. *The Content of Faith: The Best of Karl Rahner's Theological Writings.* New York: Crossroads.

_____. 1981. *Prayers and Meditations.* John Griffitus, ed. New York: Crossroads.

Rilke, Rainer Maria. 1993. *Duino Elegres.* Stephen Mitchell, trans. Boston: Shambhala.

_____. 1963. *Stories of God.* M. D. Herder, trans. New York: W. W. Norton.

Rinpoche, Sogyal. 1992. *The Tibetan Book of Living and Dying.* San Francisco: Harper Collins.

Robinson, Roxana. 1989. *Georgia O'Keefe, A Life.* New York: Harper and Row.

Rosenthal, Ted. 1973. *How Could I Not Be Among You?* New York: George Braziller.

Salinger, J. D. 1984. *The Catcher in the Rye.* New York: Phoenix Press.

_____. 1961. *Franny and Zooey.* Boston: Little Brown.

Schillebeeck, Edward. 1980. *The Experience of Jesus as Lord.* John Bowden, trans. New York: The Seabury Press.

Scott-Maxwell, Florida. 1979. *The Measure of My Days.* New York: Penguin.

Shakespeare, William. 1911. *The Complete Works of William Shakespeare.* Aldis Wright, ed. New York: Grosset and Dunlap.

Shilibu, Murasaki. 1981. *The Tale of the Genji.* Edward G. Seidensticker, ed. New York: Alfred A. Knopf.

Sinetar, Marsha. 1986. *Ordinary People as Monks and Mystics.* New York: Paulist Press.

Singer, June. 1988. *A Gnostic Book of Hours.* San Francisco: Harper and Collins.

Stroud, Joanne H. 1994. *The Bonding of Will and Desire*. New York: Continuum.

Toner, Jules J. 1982. *A Commentary on St. Ignatius' Rules for the Discernment of Spirits*. St. Louis, Mo.: The Institute of Jesuit Sources.

Underhill, Evelyn. 1974. *Mysticism*. New York: American Library.

Vanier, Jean. 1970. *Tears of Silence*. Denville, N.J.: Dimension Books.

Waddell, Helen. 1998. *The Desert Fathers: Translations from the Latin*. New York: Vintage Books.

_____. 1932. *Peter Abelard*. New York: Henry Holt.

Walker, Alice. 1983. *In Search of Our Mothers' Gardens*. San Diego: Harcourt Brace Jovanovich.

Watts, Alan. 1978. *Uncarved Block, Unbleached Silk*. New York: A & T.

Wheatley, Margaret J. 1994. *Leadership and the New Science*. San Francisco: Berrett-Koehler.

Wheatley, Margaret J. and Myron Kellner-Rogers. 1996. *A Simpler Way*. San Francisco: Berrett-Koehler.

Wheelwright, Jane Hollister. 1990. *For Women Growing Older: The Animus*. Houston, Tx. The C. G. Jung Center.

Wilde, Oscar. 1974. *The Picture of Dorian Gray*. Isobel Murray, ed. London: Oxford University Press.

Dr. Ira Progoff's Philosophy of Holistic Depth Psychology and the Progoff *Intensive Journal*® Program

Progoff *Intensive Journal*® method is an integrated system of writing exercises that is designed to help individuals develop their lives in an ongoing way. The method implements, in a practical way, Progoff's theories of depth psychology that he developed as a psychotherapist, university-based research professor, scholar on the theories of Dr. Carl Jung and author and lecturer.

Progoff's approach to psychology is unique, going against the grain of traditional clinical and academic psychology. He emphasized that the ultimate task is to help individuals grow by reconnecting them at an inner level with the sustaining and creative forces of life. He believed in the vast creative and spiritual potential of the human spirit. He did not believe in diagnosing people but rather viewed their problems as being caused by their creative processes being blocked. The key objective of psychology is to reactivate the process of growth so that individuals can expand their capacities and overcome the blockages to realize their potential.

As a depth psychologist, Progoff believed that personal and spiritual development occurs by working at an inner level, at one's depths, the creative component of individuality. He emphasized the need to provide ways of direct experience by which each person could find greater meaning since it can only happen by persons verifying it for themselves.

Progoff viewed life as an ongoing process, moving through cycles or phases of change over time in a manner analogous to the seasons of nature. Progoff's approach seeks to evoke or draw forth the potentiality and capacities in individuals, as opposed to analyzing their situation which stops the continuity of growth.

Progoff referred to his specific theories of depth psychology as holistic depth psychology. "Holistic" refers to the qualitative evolution of persons that occurs when individuals' experiences come together to form new "holes" or units, a concept that was originally developed by Jan Christian Smuts. Working at a depth level, individuals are reaching toward greater wholeness or development of their true seed nature.

Given these central principles of self-development, Progoff developed the *Intensive Journal®* method beginning in 1966 to serve as a flexible means of objectifying the organic process by which the growth of personality proceeds. Designed with minimal terminology, these procedures provide individuals with the means for moving directly into their inner process and drawing forth emotions and experiences to make them accessible and tangible for further development. The structure of sections and corresponding writing exercises mirror the subjective process taking place within personality development that Progoff found to exist based upon his research on the lives of creative persons.

The *Intensive Journal®* method utilizes a structured approach, with exercises for each area of a person's life. There are "log" sections in which participants record through brief entries the factual data of their lives. The "feedback" sections contain the active exercises that generate energy and transformation of awareness.

The *Intensive Journal®* workbook is divided into four primary areas or "dimensions of experience," each of which has a unique content and characteristics of expression. Each dimension then contains more defined areas of focus, or mini-sections.

Life/Time Dimension – The *Life/Time Dimension* contains all of our experiences that cumulatively form our personal life history. This includes both the outer experiences of a person's life history that occur in objective or chronological time and our inner or subjective perception of our life history in qualitative time. A major goal is to gain a greater sense of the continuity and context of our lives as a basis for our future decisions.

Dialogue Dimension – In the *Dialogue Dimension*, we deepen our relationship to major areas of our lives. Progoff views each of these areas as a person, having a life history with a unique seed potential which we can enter into and enhance our relationship and understanding through a dialogue exercise.

Depth Dimension – The *Depth Dimension* covers those aspects of our lives that are experienced in symbolic terms: dreams and imagery. The deeper-than-conscious contains levels of awareness that may provide valuable leads for the development of our lives. Progoff's unique non-analytical methods allow for the flow of new thoughts, ideas, intuitions and awareness from the deeper-than-conscious.

Meaning Dimension – The *Meaning Dimension* or *Process Meditation*™ *Dimension*, provides an integrated set of procedures for deepening inner experience in the context of individuals' entire spiritual lives. This ongoing spiritual discipline is designed to foster greater meaning in life, for developing and clarifying values, priorities, beliefs, areas of ultimate concern, and experiences of connection.

The structure of the *Intensive Journal*® workbook offers several advantages. It provides an organized way for participants to gain a foundation on the many different areas of their lives. It implements Progoff's broad-based "Whole-Life" approach, for working in a wide range of life experiences to create a foundation for making decisions, which adds to a person's perspective. Issues can be viewed in a larger context and become more manageable, providing a protection from premature judgments, thereby enhancing its safety.

Unlike a diary where the writer is passively recording their entries, writing in the *Intensive Journal®* workbook is an active and cumulative process. Through the *Journal Feedback™* process, participants avoid self-conscious analysis and preconceived ways of thinking to overcome blockages and foster breakthroughs. Issues are viewed from different angles to realize connections and thereby create integrations of awareness. Progoff emphasized that growth is a continuous or cumulative process, with a broad focus on one's life as a whole. Without this commitment, the continuity of the life is lost and there is no integration.

The best way to learn the method is by attending an *Intensive Journal®* workshop. A certified leader under the auspices of Dr. Progoff's organization, Dialogue House Associates, guides participants step-by-step through the exercises. The power of the group atmosphere provides an energy and discipline for each person to work privately in their own lives. The progressive deepening atmosphere of the workshop that develops over time helps participants work at deeper levels, as they become more removed from their daily lives and preconceived ways of thinking.

The workshop is set in a contemplative atmosphere where participants are writing about their lives in a deepening silence, which is conducive for inner work. Within the group, privacy is an important aspect of the method. Participants' privacy is respected for them to feel safe and to be honest with themselves. No one comments on another participant's life.

People of different backgrounds and interests attend the *Intensive Journal®* program with the overall goal of developing more meaningful lives. They may attend to learn a technique for gaining a perspective on the direction of their life and a foundation for future decisions. Participants gain insights about different areas of their lives such as personal relationships, career/hobbies, body and health, and important or dramatic events. People who are in transition have found the method especially valuable. Given Dr. Progoff's emphasis upon spiritual development as an overall component of self-growth, the method has enjoyed a strong following among various religious denominations.

It is not necessary to like to or be able to write well; participants are the only ones who read the material that they write. They are not writing a story about their lives, but rather, the writing process provides a means to make a person's experiences tangible so that they can be developed.

Dr. Progoff's book, *At a Journal Workshop: Writing to Access the Power of the Unconscious and Evoke Creative Ability* (rev. ed. 1992) provides a description of each *Intensive Journal*® exercise and the principles of depth psychology behind the method. The book serves as a useful resource for being introduced to the general goals and principles of the method as well as to learn more about working in specific exercises after a workshop. This book was selected by *Common Boundary Magazine* as "one of the 65 most significant books on psychology and spirituality of the 20th century."

Dialogue House is an approved provider of continuing education in counseling, social work and related areas. Please contact Dialogue House for information about the professional benefits to be derived from attending the programs as well as specific organizations with which it is an approved provider.

For more information about Dr. Progoff's programs and materials, please contact Dialogue House Associates, 799 Broadway, Suite 519, New York, NY 10003-6811. Telephone: 212-673-5880 / 800-221-5844. www.intensivejournal.org. Email: info@intensivejournal.org.

"Intensive Journal" (registered) and "Journal Feedback," "Progoff," and "Process Meditation" are trademarks of Ira Progoff and are used under license by Dialogue House Associates.

How to Use the Enhanced CD

The Enhanced CD contains 13 audio tracks that will play on any CD player. In addition, this CD contains a video file that will play on a computer.

For PCs

Your Enhanced CD will open automatically when the AutoPlay feature of Windows is enabled. If the AutoPlay feature is disabled, follow these instructions:

1 Insert your Enhanced CD in the CD-ROM drive.

2 From the Windows desktop, double-click on the My Computer drive.

3 Double-click the icon representing your computer's CD-ROM drive.

4 Double-click the icon titled IRENE_DUGAN_REMEMBERED to open the file for viewing.

The audio portion of the CD may also be heard on your computer using Windows Media Player.

For Macintosh

1 Insert your Enhanced CD in the CD-ROM drive. An icon titled IRENE_DUGAN_REMEMBERED will appear on the desktop. Open that icon.

2 Double-click on the title to open the file for playback using QuickTime.

The audio portion of the CD may also be heard on your computer using iTunes or QuickTime.

Love Is All Around in Disguise:
Meditations for Spiritual Seekers

Compact Disc Track Identifications

Track 1: Irene Dugan, r.c.: In Her Own Words

Track 2: Thoughts on the Dugan Spiritual Legacy

Track 3: Using a Journal

Track 4: A Centering Experience (Introduction)

Track 5: A Guide to Entering Inner Stillness (Chapter 2)

Track 6: Noticing: Introduction to the Kairos Biography
(Chapter 2)

Track 7: The Kairos Biography: A Guided Meditation (Chapter 2)

Track 8: Incarnational Spirituality: Introduction to
Contemplation (Chapter 3)

Track 9: A Guided Contemplation (Chapter 3)

Track 10: Using Mantras in Meditation (Chapter 6)

Track 11: Some Questions to Ponder

Track 12: A Guided Meditation: Creating a Mantra from
Life Experience (Chapter 6)

Track 13: Words of Trust from Prophets (Chapter 6)

Video File: "Irene Dugan Remembered" – A Visual Portrait

The improvised piano music that weaves through the CD is from *Songs of the Soul: Music from Within* by Jerri E. Greer. Dr. Greer composed this music between 1992 and 1997 as part of her own process of finding voice for her soul's longing for expression. Dr. Greer is the founder of Pathways, which offers programs exploring Jungian psychology, spirituality and the arts. Her CD *Songs of the Soul: Music from Within* may be ordered from Pathways, P.O. Box 222, Flossmoor, IL 60422, for $15, which includes postage and handling.

About the Author

Avis Clendenen is Professor of Religious Studies at Saint Xavier University and adjunct Professor of Pastoral Theology at Catholic Theological Union in Chicago. She holds her Ph.D. in Theology and the Human Sciences from Chicago Theological Seminary where she also received a Doctor of Ministry degree. She is the editor of *Spirituality in Depth: Essays in Honor of Sister Irene Dugan, r.c.* (Chiron Publications, 2002) and is co-author with Troy W. Martin of *Forgiveness: Finding Freedom Through Reconciliation* (Crossroad Publications, 2002).

Index